Griswold
Point

Griswold Point

.... HISTORY FROM ....
THE MOUTH OF THE CONNECTICUT RIVER

WICK GRISWOLD

Charleston | London

THE
History
PRESS

Published by The History Press
Charleston, SC 29403
www.historypress.net

First published 2014

Manufactured in the United States

ISBN 978.1.62619.571.4

Library of Congress CIP data applied for.

CONTENTS

Contents

ACKNOWLEDGEMENTS

This project has been a labor of love on the part of many people connected to Griswold Point, the Connecticut River and Connecticut history. I would like to offer my heartfelt thanks to all involved for their knowledge, insights, efforts, time and energy. Griswold Point is a special place, and it plays a special role in the history of Connecticut and our country. But it is really the people it engenders that make it so very special. So thanks can never really be given enough times to enough people. But here it goes, anyway.

Scads and scads of gratitude must go to Suki Schavoir for her patience, expertise and willingness to put up with my nonsense. Thank you, Suki—your talents in graphic design are matched only by your helpfulness and cheerful attitude. Her brother, Frederick, also deserves a round of applause for his artwork, friendship, ping-pong table and willingness to share his extensive knowledge of Griswold Point, the Black Hall River, the Connecticut River and Long Island Sound. Their wonderful mother, Shelby, should be applauded for having such great offspring and for her willingness to share the research materials that she and her late husband, Peter, so painstakingly tweaked out of family history and lore.

Matthew Griswold X was most helpful in terms of initiating the project and sharing family stories and providing insight into the work of his father and "the Aunties." Peter, Tim, Sloane, Mark, Evan, Caroline, Emily, Betsy, Sarah and Yvonne Griswold; Emily Fisher; and Jennifer Hillhouse were ongoing inspirations, fonts of knowledge and sources of good cheer and helpfulness.

Special thanks also to Helena Ostafin and 'Bama Bill for creating the perfect creative environment at Joe's House. Murray, Adela and Lucius Wilmerding deserve many thanks for sharing their photographs and hospitality. Anne Bingham Pierson not only provided research material but also reinforced the idea that successful men are usually supported by strong, capable women. And thanks to Beth Nelligan for being so strong and capable.

The splendid cadre of photographers requires a few huzzahs, too. Carla Griswold Giorgio, Jeff Feldmann, Ray and Annette Guasp and Stephan Bullard, please put down your cameras for a second and take a well-deserved bow.

The editorial and marketing crew at The History Press are, as always, just stellar. I'd like to thank Dani McGrath for all her hard work and the daily Facebook fun. Tabitha Dulla was absolutely spot-on in keeping the whole lightly serious process rolling. I thank her for her patience and understanding. Also, thanks to Jeff Saraceno for getting the ball rolling. Best of luck to you, Jeff—hope to see you in New Britain sometime.

The administrative and support team at the University of Hartford must be thanked for their flexibility, creativity and support. Deans David Goldenberg and Woody Doane went above and beyond with their support and friendship. Thanks, guys. Go Yanks! Bonny Taylor, you are just the best!

Sierra Dixon of the Connecticut Historical Society gets a well-deserved shout-out for her expeditious assistance, warmth and kindness. Nicole Wholean and Matt Green at the Florence Griswold Museum were also warm, kind and helpful. Annita Andrick of the Erie County Historical Society was also exceedingly helpful with information about the Pennsylvania Griswolds. As always, Amy Trout of the Connecticut River Museum and Jacqueline Talbot, catalyst and muse at the Connecticut River Watershed Council, lent their much-appreciated support to this effort.

I must also express the sincerest of thanks and the warmest of love to Annie Griswold, whose love, understanding and ability to weave a tapestry of sensibility out of times of transition can never be adequately appreciated. Oh yes, and also to you, Maggie Mae (the Bulldozer), for dragging me on all those walks to the beach, where much of the soul of Griswold Point is to be discovered. Again, thanks to all. I wish you the very best.

Chapter 1

GRISWOLD POINT
INTRODUCTION

At the beginning of the second decade of the twenty-first century, the barrier beach that protects the marshes where the Connecticut River meets Long Island Sound was buffeted and blasted by Tropical Storm Irene and Super Storm Sandy. As a result, the spit of land known as Griswold Point (41° 16' 45" North, 72° 19' 46" West) was breached in several places and now, at high tide, it is an island rather than a point. The geomorphic changes it has undergone are, in a very real sense, metaphors for the historical, cultural and social changes that the people who have lived there for thousands of years have experienced. Griswold Point is an excellent model for understanding the time and tide-washed transformations that resonate down from paleo-people through the colonists, Revolutionaries, Federalists, shipbuilders, clipper captains, Civil War heroes, captains of industry, entrepreneurs, inventors, barrage balloonists and, finally, the environmentalists of today. Griswold Point provides a canvas on which is painted a panorama of the unfolding American story that can be seen in terms of conquest, cultivation, commerce and culture.

The indigenous people known at the Nehantics, whose name means "of long-necked waters," presumably derived from the long neck of Griswold Point, occupied the region for a few thousand years prior to the arrival of the Dutch and the English. The area's location made it an ideal habitat for gathering fish and shellfish, including the clams whose shells were drilled and polished to make wampum, the storytelling currency that formed an important focus of native cultural life. The land was arable and could be

Aerial view of Griswold Point, circa 1950s. Note that the point extends to the Connecticut River and has not been significantly breached. *Griswold family archives*.

farmed for pumpkins, squash, beans and the all-important corn, which was the backbone of sustenance and trade up and down the Connecticut River and Long Island Sound. Deer were (and still are) also plentiful. The rich biodiversity of the region's marshes and forests provided abundant hunting and foraging opportunities. In short, the area now known as Griswold Point was able to sustain a stable population of people for several millennia up until the Pequots and the Europeans appeared in the area to change the human ecology forever. The Pequots, whose name means "the destroyers," were a bellicose band of interlopers who had been driven out of what is now New York State because of their unsociable and warlike ways and lack of regard for the lives and territories of other native groups. Their arrival on the Connecticut River changed forever the loose alliances of the Algonquin-speaking River Indians who lived between the sound and the Enfield Rapids. The River Indians were a relatively peaceful lot and were overwhelmed by the ferocity of the Pequots. The Pequots established their main base a few miles east of Nehantic territory and routinely terrorized the people who lived on the river and sound. As we shall see, the area around the point and its early European residents played an important role in the extirpation of the Pequots and Nehantics and the establishment of a permanent, colonial, Anglo-Saxon society.

Even more devastating than the Pequots to the Nehantic way of life was the European invasion and colonization of the lower Connecticut River Valley. The Dutch captain Adrian Block sailed the *Onrust* (Restless) into the mouth of the river in 1614. One of the theories as to the name Black Hall, which is what the area around Griswold Point is called, is that it was originally called Block's Hole because it was where the Dutch trader and explorer anchored during his first night on the river. As we shall see, several other theories about the origin of the Black Hall name still abound. Captain Block returned to Holland with tales of a river that was teeming with beaver, mink, otter and other valuable fur-bearing animals. He reported that the natives were friendly and easily manipulated and duped. As a result, the Dutch established a trading post fifty miles upstream of the point at present-day Hartford. They also erected a ramshackle fort on the west side of the river's mouth, on the opposite shore from the finger of land that ultimately became known as Griswold Point. The Dutch called their little piece of land Kviet's Hook, which translates to "Plover's Corner" in English. Interestingly, the preservation of the endangered piping plover is still a major environmental concern in the area today.

The Dutch were eventually driven off the river by the agriculturally minded English after several decades of mostly bloodless confrontations. It was the English occupation of the mouth of the river that set into motion the concatenation of events that still resonate on Griswold Point at the present almost four centuries later. The English would come to control the flow of traffic in and out of the river and secure the area militarily. It was within the parameters of that security and control of the territory that the stage was set for the arrival of the Griswold family and its centuries-long residency at the point where the Connecticut River meets Long Island Sound.

It is helpful to put the history of Griswold Point into a socio-cultural context. A useful framework of analysis is to look at it in terms of the major institutions that any society must have to sustain itself and continue through time. These institutions fulfill the basic social needs that every society must meet in order to exist. The acronym FREEMMP is a convenient way of remembering what they are: Family, Religion, Economics, Education, Medicine, Military and Politics. The family is necessary for procreation and sustaining dependent children. Families also determine who can do what to whom, which is always a concern where gene pools are small. Some form of religion is necessary to answer the three unanswerable questions: Where did we come from? Who are we? Where are we going? Religions are also useful in providing social control. Economics must provide its members with food, water goods and services. Education is how a society passes on its survival strategies and identities. Medicine keeps people healthy. A military is essential for defense and territorial expansion when needed. Lastly, every society must have a political system to provide order among its members. Taken all together, these institutions give every society its form, content and meaning. The Griswold family has excelled at all of these.

It was religion, economics and politics that ultimately led the Griswold family to their Point. Early seventeenth-century England was a cauldron of chaotic military turmoil with political and religious factions fighting for power and treasure. Roundheads and Royalists, Protestants and Catholics, Kings and Parliaments aligned against one another in constant states of turmoil and conflict. In order to escape this instability, and its dangers, a group of gentlemen under the auspices of Lord Saye and Sele and Lord Brook obtained a patent from the Earl of Warwick that gave them control of much of what is now the Connecticut coastline and river valley. Exactly how the earl was entitled to give away what had been home to the Nehantics and other tribes for ages was never clearly explained. But given their superior firepower over the natives and the Dutch, the English lords decided that they were going to create a "Paradise for Gentlemen" at the mouth of the river that the Indians knew as the Quinneckitikut. This word, from which "Connecticut" descended, is commonly believed to mean "the long tidal river." But since there is no word for "tidal" in Algonquin, it means the "Long River."

To enforce their claim to the territory, the lords hired a Dutch military engineer named Lion Gardiner to kick out the Dutch and build a real fort at the mouth of the river with "greate gunnes" and other weapons of mass destruction. The fort was named Saybrook in honor of its noble sponsors. These weapons would eventually be used to eliminate the Pequots from the river and sound, thus ending their reign of terror and making the land safe for English settlement, agriculture and trade. Once the fort was established, the Dutch booted off the river and the Pequots purged, Lion Gardiner was rewarded with an island off the coast of New York that still bears his family name. With his retirement from public life, the scene was set for the entrance of the Griswold family, who would play an important role in the unfolding dramas of the nascent colony of Connecticut. One of the scenes in that drama has a beautiful, young Griswold lady being blown ashore by a gale on

The Black X Line ship *Toronto* under full sail. *Griswold family archives.*

Gardiner's Island, a shipwreck that resulted in romance and the combining of dynasties…but more of that later.

The catalyst and muse who inspired and resulted in Griswold Point was the legendary beauty Lady Fenwick. Colonel George Fenwick was the only English gentleman who actually came to the paradise envisioned by Lords Saye and Sele and Brook. George Fenwick sailed from England with his lovely bride, Lady Alice, in 1637 and became the chief administrator of the Saybrook Colony. His wife is the ultimate archetype of the pioneering European woman who crossed the Atlantic to tame the savage land and turn it into a fecund enticement for others to follow in her wake. She was an excellent herbalist and horticulturalist, a crack shot, a world-class equestrian, an accomplished rower, a dulcet-toned singer of madrigals, a warm and cheerful mother, a loving wife and a thrifty housekeeper—and she was drop-dead gorgeous, to boot. Her untimely death, shortly after the birth of her second child, was the seminal event that brought the Griswolds to their Point. I hope you will find the story of the Griswold family interesting. The family certainly played an important role in early colonial history. They took a strong part in the Revolutionary War, the War of 1812, the Civil War, the World Wars and some that came later. They were part of the Manifest Destiny of the United States. Their ships navigated all the oceans of the world in the expansion of American commerce. They provided Connecticut and the fledgling United States with some of their greatest early statesmen. They forged the pots and pans that fed the westward migration. Theirs, in a very real sense, is the story of America as its culture and society continues to evolve.

Chapter 2

THE ENGLISH CONNECTION

The genetic odyssey that became the Griswold family in Old Lyme, Connecticut, begins in England in the area known in family lore as "the Griswold Triangle" It extends from Birmingham at its northern apex to Cubbington in the east and Shakespeare's Stratford-on-Avon at its southern tip. It is near the Bard's birthplace that the first know reference to the family can be traced. There is record of a Griswold family (undoubtedly with one of the variant spellings of the name) in Snitterfield, a borough of Stratford-upon-Avon as early as 1226. Available source documents affirm that there were many Griswold families in the triangle region in the fourteenth and fifteenth centuries.

William de Grousewold was listed as living in Kynton Lyndon in 1332 and was noted as the chaplain of St. Alphege Church in Solihull in 1349. A John Greswold married the daughter of William Hugford of Hulverly Hall sometime around 1300. Thomas Griswold was recognized as "Clerk of the Crown in the Court of the King's Bench from October of 1422 to July of 1458." He was also the "Filazer" of Warwickshire from 1418 until his death. A filazer is essentially someone who keeps records. Thomas was described as "Lord of the Manor" at Pemberton and was noted for his generosity to the church.

Not all the Griswolds in England were well-to-do, though. Richard Gryswolde couldn't pay his "paricherentes" in 1591, and one Henry Greswolde was publicly listed as being on the dole. Most of the Griswolds, however, were property owners and virtually all of them farmers, to greater or lesser degrees.

A main branch of the family eventually settled at Malvern Hall and became prosperous landowners. The agricultural skills passed on from generation to generation in England left the pioneers who emigrated to North America in good stead as they attempted to hew a living out of their new world.

As we have seen, there were several ways the family surname was spelled. English records show it at various times as Greswold, Greswolde, Griswald, Griswold, Greswould, Griswould, Gryswold, Gryswolde, Gryssole, Grissolde, Grissold, de Greswold, de Grosewold, Grisold, Gresnold, Grizzil and Grizwold. By the time the family crossed the Atlantic, the spelling was trending toward the Griswold of today. There are several speculations as to the derivation of the name. English names in the past usually came from an association with a place or an occupation. One theory is that Griswold originated from "greosn," the Old English word for "gravel and wold," which was an open piece of uncultivated land. If this were the case, the Griswolds hailed from a gravelly break in the forest, which must have been a challenge to their agricultural skills.

Other conjectures are focused on the Old English word for "pig," which was "gris." That would mean that the name means "those who dwell in woods frequented by pigs." This is a favorite among family members today when they are in a jocular mood. Other guesses include "gray wood," based on the French name for that color. A theory that is growing in popularity in the twenty-first century is that is derives from the Icelandic "grey," which means dog. This would be in keeping with the running greyhounds that decorate the family coat of arms. King Edward I said that of all his dogs, he was fondest of the greyhounds raised by the Griswolds of Solihul. He also commended them for their bravery in fighting the Crusades.

It is believed that the Griswold coat of arms is directly related to their breeding of royal greyhounds and participation in the Crusades. The crest always features running hounds. The motto used by the Old Lyme branch of the family is *Fortiter et Celeriter*, which loosely translates as "Bravely and Swiftly" or "Strongly and Swiftly." Other branches of the family, while keeping the same dog graphics, have different mottos, such as *Palmam Qui Meruit Ferat*, which means "They who earn the palm should bear it." It was the motto inscribed on the funeral car of Lord Nelson and is also the motto of the University of Southern California. The other motto associated with the Griswold crest is *Vonando Reptilia Spernum*, which translates into "Flying, I spurn those that creep." Family lore has it that along with keeping greyhounds, Griswolds were royal messengers. The use of *Celeriter* and

The Griswold coat of arms features running greyhounds and the motto *Fortier and Celeriter*.
Photo by Ray Guasp.

Vonando in their mottos might bear out this long-standing belief. Griswold greyhounds can be found to this day on the badge of Solihull School and the shield of the Burough of Solihull.

It was religious and political turmoil that motivated the Griswolds to leave their ancestral homes and venture across the Atlantic in search of a more amenable social climate. Robert Greville inherited the title of Lord Brook. Oxford educated, Brook traveled extensively throughout Europe. He married into the anti-Royalist Russell family, which further solidified his political stance against the Crown. He became a member of Parliament from Warwick. He was increasingly distressed by the iniquities arising after the beginning of the reign of Charles I. He teamed up with William Fiennes, the Viscount of Saye and Sele, an important member of Parliament, to develop a scheme "to quit England and settle in some part of the world where Kings and Court should be unknown."

These scions of the nobility collaborated with Robert Rich, the Earl of Warwick, who granted them a large tract of land in what became known as Connecticut. The Earl had received ownership of the land by a grant from the Crown in 1635. The indigenous people who lived there, as well as the Dutch, who recently established trading facilities there, disputed the Earl's claim to the real estate, but the "great gunnes" of the English reinforced his claim. Plans were laid to create a paradise for gentlemen (and, presumably, their wives and retainers) at the mouth of the Connecticut River. However, the political climate in England changed dramatically, and Lord Saye and Sele and Lord Brooke abandoned their utopian quest.

However, they did commission, as we have seen, Lion Gardiner to build a fort where the river debouches into Long Island Sound. This fort served the dual purpose of eliminating the murderous Pequot Indians as a military threat and driving the Dutch off the river permanently. Rewarded with an island of his own off the shores of Long Island, Gardiner retired from Connecticut, setting the stage for the arrival of Colonel George Fenwick and his remarkable wife. Fenwick was the only member of the British nobility to actually make it to Saybrook. His selection of Matthew Griswold as his deputy governor set the stage for the extraordinary saga of the Griswold family in Old Lyme and beyond.

The castle of Viscount Saye and Sele was in the Warwick region, as was the home of Lord Brooke. The area was a hotbed of Puritan revolutionary activity, and the Reverend Ephraim Huit was at the center of the controversy. He was out of favor with the upper echelons of church hierarchy, especially his bishop. Since things were getting too hot for him in

England, he was selected to be the leader of a contingent of emigrants who were to implement the plans of Saye and Sele and Brooke. He also counted members of the Griswold family among his congregants, and through this connection, Edward and Matthew Griswold were persuaded to further their fortunes in the wilderness of North America, as their cousin Francis had a few years earlier.

Chapter 3
MATTHEW I

The progenitor of the Griswold family at Griswold Point is Matthew I. He was born in Kenilworth, Warwickshire, England, sometime between 1615 and 1622. His Puritan inclinations and sense of adventure led him across the Atlantic Ocean in the ship *Christian* as part of the "Winthrop Fleet." In 1639, after a sojourn at Dorchester in the Massachusetts Colony, he accompanied the Reverend Ephraim Huit up the Connecticut River and established himself in the settlement called Windsor. There, he wooed and won Anna Wolcott, daughter of one of Connecticut's most prominent early settlers, Henry Wolcott. They were married in 1646. The young couple soon moved down the Connecticut to the mouth of the river, where they met their destiny in the fledgling colony.

Matthew was a lawyer and a stonecutter; both occupations served him well in the nascent colony. He was appointed as the agent and deputy of Colonel George Fenwick, the successor to Lion Gardiner as the governor of the Saybrook Colony. Fenwick and his small entourage occupied Fort Saybrook at the mouth of the river, where they farmed corn, traded with the natives up and down the river and, most importantly, controlled river commerce in and out of Long Island Sound. Life at the fort could be difficult at times. Harsh winters and dry summers posed challenges. When supply ships failed to arrive from England, economic circumstances and supplies could get a bit tight. But the colony survived and prospered. The quality of life at the fort and its environs was greatly enhanced by the skills and energy of Fenwick's wife, who played a key role in the development of Griswold Point.

Matthew Griswold carved this tomb for his father-in-law, Henry Wolcott. He shipped the Portland brownstone upriver to Windsor on a barge. *Photo by Carla Griswold Giorgio.*

Lady Alice Fenwick (she was a Lady due to a brief marriage in England to Sir John Boteler, who left his bride a widow at a young age) was a remarkable person. In many ways, she is the personification of the pioneer women who emigrated across the ocean and pushed relentlessly westward, carving farms and homesteads out of wildernesses filled with unfamiliar animals and people whose cultures were wildly divergent from their own. She married Colonel Fenwick, who was the only member of the aristocracy associated with Lords Saye and Sele and Brook to actually make it to the lands granted by the Warwick Patents. Lady Fenwick eagerly agreed to accompany her husband on his overseas adventure to help him settle and govern the Saybrook Colony.

And help him she did. Lady Fenwick was instrumental in improving the lives and lifestyles of both the English and the Indians in the Saybrook area. On her voyage to Connecticut, she brought with her seeds and cuttings of all the plants from her garden back in England. She vowed to transplant them and nurture them in their new environment. One might wonder if this is what inspired Colonel Fenwick to declare the new colony's motto to be *Qui*

Transtulit Sustinet (Those Transplanted Shall Sustain). The seal he designed to go with the motto displayed nine grape vines, perhaps like those his wife brought over from Britain. Her garden at the fort became a locally famous paragon of food production and healing botanicals. She was an excellent horticulturalist and was adept at creating plant-based poultices and potions based on ancient European lore and the local knowledge of the Indians.

Not only could she garden, but she also was a crack shot, a superb equestrian and a power rower. She communicated well with the area Indians and was also a very good singer. And to top in all off, people who wrote about her usually remarked on her lovely face, comely figure and lustrous, long, flaxen hair. Her homesteading skills were greatly appreciated by those out on the west shore of the river's mouth. One of the challenges she faced was the lack of convivial female companionship. There weren't many European women in the colony; however, she was able to form a bond with Anna Wolcott Griswold. The women enjoyed rowing on the river together while singing madrigals. Since the church was in Harford, Lady Fenwick brought her two children upstream in order for them to be baptized. Anna Wolcott Griswold and many others were shocked and saddened by Lady Fenwick's unexpected death in 1645. The Saybrook Colony was never the same. Colonel Fenwick consolidated its political entity with the Connecticut Colony, at which time it ceased to exist as a unit of governance. Inconsolable after the death of his inspired wife, Fenwick closed out his affairs in North America and sailed back to England to fight against King Charles. When Fenwick sailed for England, Matthew was left in Connecticut with the major responsibilities that accompanied governing the Saybrook area. He carried them out dutifully, and they remain an important part of his legacy even as the twenty-first century slips into it teenaged years.

Matthew was charged by Colonel Fenwick to place a stone over Lady Fenwick's grave and to care for it in perpetuity. Mathew certainly lived up to that obligation. He constructed or hired a barge capable of carrying some weight and pushed and pulled it up the river to the Portland area. There, his skills as a stonecutter came into play. He quarried out at least three large blocks of the malleable rock that is now known as Portland Brownstone. One of these stones he then hewed into the monument that would mark Lady Fenwick's final destination. The other stones became the markers for his father-in-law, Henry Wolcott, and his mother-in-law, Elizabeth, in Windsor. He also fashioned one for George Wyllys, the third governor of Connecticut, in the Ancient Burying Ground at Hartford. All three stones are still fulfilling their function almost four hundred years after the pioneering Griswold

Elizabeth Wolcott was one of the first English women in Connecticut. *Photo by Carla Griswold Giorgio.*

Matthew Griswold also carved this tomb for George Wyllys, an early governor of Connecticut. It can still be found in Hartford's Ancient Burying Ground. *Photo by Jeff Feldmann.*

Matthew Griswold X, his son and his grandson keeping the family pledge to maintain the tomb of Lady Fenwick. Many family members help out with this effort. *Photo by Abigail Phieffer, courtesy of the* New London Day.

Black Hall River Bridge, circa 1900. *Griswold family archives.*

crafted them. The Griswold family still sees to the maintenance of Lady Fenwick's grave.

Matthew was well rewarded for his efforts on Colonel Fenwick's behalf, receiving seven pounds sterling, a nice monetary remuneration. More germane to his ongoing legacy, however, Fenwick rewarded Griswold with a very large tract of land from the Warwick Patent that covered what family members estimate was more than ten thousand acres on the eastern mouth of the Connecticut River, extending from present-day Old Lyme to New London. There, Matthew established his estate, which quickly became known as Black Hall. There are several explanations for the name "Black Hall," the most historically satisfying being that is an elision of "Block's Hole," which would connect it to the very first European contact with the area. Some say it was named for a baronial estate in England or a religious site known as Blackfriar's Hall. There is a persistent, if discredited, rationale that falsely assumes Matthew sent one of Fenwick's slaves or servants over to occupy the territory because a person of color would be more welcomed by the Indians than a "paleface." The fable says that Matthew built a log cabin, and the building was called Black's Hall. It is here that the story falls apart, as the English almost never built log structures.

Whatever the origin of its name, Black Hall was cultivated and improved by Matthew, who began to turn it from wilderness into productive farming and fishing territory. Matthew Griswold I was an important personage in the new colony. He was a magistrate, a justice of the peace, a lieutenant in the Train Band, a horse trader, a farmer and the deputy governor of the Saybrook Colony. He exhibited the Renaissance man's ability to master a large number of skills and an eclectic base of knowledge and to apply them to the practical ends of creating an estate that still continues to this day. He was a person of thought as well as a person of action. Just as he hewed monuments from stone, he wrested a life and a lifestyle from the land with focused application of his intellect and muscle. He also kept a relationship with a religious community. He was a lifelong member of the Saybrook Congregational Church. He presented the church with its first silver cup to be used in communion. It was inscribed "S.C. Ex Domini Matthai Griswold." The "S.C." is believed to stand for *Sacramentalis Calix*.

There is a quaint, yet telling, description of Matthew in a 1935 publication, *The Griswold Family in America: The 1ˢᵗ Five Generations*:

Matthew was a typical Englishman, hardy and venturesome, with a lusty desire to accumulate large landholdings, and with a vigorous method of accomplishing it. He was held in high esteem by the early settlers, and was a counselor and friend to all. He possessed very largely those traits of physique and character so often met with in men of the Griswold clan. He had a large community spirit, was genial and easy going, yet forceful when required. He was a man of powerful build who used his strength in combat with the wilderness to found a home and fortune, while being exceedingly kind and gentle with his family.

In the spirit of family kindness, Matthew was an early champion of women's rights in the Connecticut Colony. Anna inherited twelve "akers" of land in the Great Meadow of Windsor upon the death of her brother. It was the legal and social custom of the time that women whose husbands were living could not own property. Matthew flew in the face of this tradition. In April 1663, he declared in court that the land should be recorded as belonging to Anna and that it should belong to her, her children and their dispose forever. This was a seminal act in terms of redefining legal gender relationships, a process that still continues. There was also gender-based legal situation that had proved to be a spot of bother for Anna and Matthew.

In 1667, Anna was accused of witchcraft by John Tillerson, a ne'er-do-well from Saybrook. Accusations of witchcraft were terrible weapons that neighbors attacked neighbors with in the middle of the seventeenth century. Tillerson was said to be jealous of Matthew's success, and he might have harbored some more personal grievances. Turnabout being fair play, Matthew had Tillerson arrested for defamation of character. The court at Saybrook fully exonerated Anna on all the charges and fined Tillerson twelve shillings (they agreed that he should have been fined more but noted that he was poor and probably couldn't pay). With accusations of witchcraft removed from her life, Anna went back to being the matriarch of her family and mistress of the manor.

Being the foremost female presence in an early colonial household must have been a daunting task at times. Starting out in a clapboard house that was a challenge to keep clean, Anna would have had to spend inordinate amounts of time cooking; baking; canning; making soap, candles and cloth; and otherwise tending to a frontier household being hewn out of the wilderness. There were also Indian neighbors to consider. Many were friendly, but some were not. It was not an easy life, but Anna's hard work was rewarded with the blessings of a devoted husband and a growing family in a beautiful part of the world.

Anna Wolcott Griswold and Matthew I became the parents of five children: Elizabeth, Anna, Matthew II, Sarah and John, all of whom grew to adulthood and became prominent citizens of the area and the state. The Griswolds became progenitors of a family that included many local, state and national judges and politicians. The family left an indelible mark on the colonial history of Connecticut and the country. Both Matthew and Anna lived very long and productive lives. He predeceased her in 1698, and she died in 1701. Their legacies and namesakes continue to the present day. As we have seen, Matthew I was a champion of women's rights; however, he wasn't the only "champion" in the family. His son Matthew II is the holder of that proud title.

Chapter 4

THE CHAMPION

M atthew II earned the honorific title of "the Champion" due to his great strength and pugilistic abilities. He was born at Black Hall in 1652 and grew to be a strapping specimen of a fellow, as quick with his wits as he was with his fists. He set about improving the properties at Black Hall, developing farming and fishing strategies that provided not only sustenance but also income. He became active in the political life of the fledgling Connecticut settlement and played key roles in the regulation of relationships between the increasing numbers of arriving English immigrants and the indigenous people they were supplanting and suppressing. He served with distinction while fighting Indians during King Phillip's War, one of the deadliest encounters per capita in our nation's history. But it was for a less bloody struggle that he earned his title and fame.

As the new colony divided itself into communities, a land dispute began to heat up between the citizens of Lyme and New London over a four-square-mile area known as Bride's Brook. Both towns claimed it, although it belonged to neither of them. Bride's Brook was originally known as Sunkipaug, but it received its Anglicized name as the result of a unique winter wedding. In 1646, a young couple from Saybrook was scheduled to be married, but the magistrate who was to perform the ceremony was prevented from officiating due to severe weather conditions. The influential colonial politician Governor John Winthrop agreed to take his place and perform the ceremony. However, treacherous icy conditions prevented him from crossing the brook to the west side, where the hopeful couple was likewise stranded.

The quick-thinking politician adapted to the situation by conducting the nuptial ritual from the east side while the happy couple recited their vows on the shores of the west bank. After being declared husband and wife, they sledded and ferried back to their home in Saybrook to begin their days of connubial bliss.

It was control of the land surrounding this brook that was the source of contention between the two young, burgeoning communities. In the spirit of equality, a petition was made to the colonial legislature to the effect that the disputed territory should be divided evenly between the two, with each town securing a claim to two square miles. The petition seemed fair enough and was approved by the solons, but when the citizens of each community met to divvy up the property, they could never come to an amicable agreement as to who was actually entitled to what. The matter came to a hostile flash point when groups of men from both towns descended on the contested meadow with sickles and scythes to trim and mow it, thereby enhancing their claims to the territory. There was a fierce and somewhat grisly skirmish, and the belligerents from both sides were arrested and fined, including the young Griswold. The New Londoners were fined five pounds, and the Lyme boys had to cough up seven pounds.

It was finally decided to settle the matter once and for all by "leaving it up to the Lord." This required each town to select two stalwart men to fight to the finish over the real estate. The last man standing would win the coveted turf for his community forever after. New London picked two muscular fellows named Hempstead and Chapman, while Lyme selected William Ely and Matthew Griswold II. The four met and fought on two occasions, and both times the Lyme battlers were victorious, with Griswold distinguishing himself in the ring. The land was given to Lyme, and Griswold returned to Black Hall to build an impressive eight-room house. The house was blown down in the hurricane of 1815, but in the interim, it served as a home to a large brood that resulted from the most fecund union between Matthew II and the lovely Phebe Hyde.

In order to initiate and facilitate this joyful and felicitous union, Matthew II had to prove himself to be a champion in the arts of wooing in addition to his prowess as a bare-knuckle brawler. Phebe was a rare treasure, and the doughty champion had his work cut out for him as he pursued her heart and her hand. She was ten years his junior, and contemporary accounts portray her as a great beauty and a bit of a "coquette." Matthew II rose to the challenge of courtship by using his way with words to compose heart-rending missives in declaration of his undying love. The result was a spate of endless stanzas of some really terrible poetry. For example: "And grant to me this token of bliss / Some lines to pen with speed / That may to me you respond / You choose me in this very deed / And if with freedom thou canst find / We may proceed to marriage bonds / And be right welcome from thy hand…" and on and on and on. However, his poesy worked, and Phebe and Matthew were married in 1683. In keeping with the need for large families, the happy couple had eleven children. Unfortunately, Phebe died relatively young at the age of forty-one. Matthew II expanded and improved his holdings at Black Hall and became a vigorous and prominent member of the Lyme community. He served in several capacities of local governance and administration. He was also pugnacious and aggressive well into his old age. When he was sixty years old, he was arrested for assaulting a man named Henry Morris with a butter churn. He beat Morris so badly that his victim was knocked out cold for several hours. He had to put up a stiff one-hundred-pound bond while he awaited trial. Found guilty, he paid the court costs of his trial and gave Morris sixteen pounds for "hurt and damage."

His numerous offspring went on to play diverse roles in colonial Connecticut and beyond. His son John, for example, was elected to the Connecticut legislature twenty-eight times and served as a judge for thirty years. Perhaps the most interesting of the lot was Matthew III, known as the "Wayward (or Prodigal) Son." His adventures read more like breathtaking fiction than real life, but history has shown that most of what he claimed befell him, actually did.

Matthew the Champion came out on the losing end of a dispute with his brother-in-law, Abraham Brunson. Brunson had married Anna, the daughter of Anna and Matthew I. He held the rank of lieutenant, but in what organization it is not known. He is reviled in family history for perpetrating an egregious rip off of the family's estates in England. He apparently served in some capacity as an executor of Matthew I's will. In the course of his work, he discovered a trunk full of papers that laid claim to ancestral properties and money in England, as well as documents that traced the family history in England. In an affidavit dated 1699, Henry Mervin alleges that Brunson had taken possession of said papers, that there were great concerns in them and that Matthew II never knew they existed—and he never should.

Matthew the Champion complained about the loss of deeds, but he did not live to see his suit successfully adjudicated. It is generally believed that the evil malice of Brunson caused the family property in England to be irretrievably lost. But what was his motivation? Why did he do it? Just out of spite? What caused such a horrendous rift between him and his brother-in-law that he would intentionally cause such damage to the family? Alas, we probably will never know. His reasons lie buried deep in the layers of centuries past. We will never know how he came into the possession of the papers in the first place or what he ultimately did with them. What we do know is that he is greatly excoriated in the family memory.

A classic example of this animosity was exemplified by one James Griswold (The Aesthete) in the nineteenth century. He used to walk from Black Hall to the Meeting House Hills and visit the ancient burying grounds there. He would camp at the grave of Abraham Bronson and exhort his ghost to appear and reveal where the papers were secreted. Unfortunately, James's sorceries came to naught, and the shade never showed up to shed light on the subject. Family members conjectured that James, who was held in high esteem by all, went to his earthly reward and may well have run into Brunson on the other side to finally satiate his curiosity.

Chapter 5

THE WAYWARD SON

That Phebe was dearly loved by Matthew the Champion is beyond doubt. Their long and fruitful marriage, along with a hearty brood of eleven offspring, is a testament to their commitment to each other. Later in his life, the Champion eulogized her as the "Godly Mother of a wayward son." The tale of this prodigal young man is one of the great adventures of the seventeenth century. His travels and travails read like an action-packed, swashbuckling saga of the sea. His exciting peregrinations took him from Griswold Point to the far corners of the Caribbean, Central and South America and Europe. His story, as recounted by his father in a letter to the famous Puritan cleric Cotton Mather, certainly was influenced by the biblical tale of the prodigal son. However, it also has its own unique twists and turns that make it a colonial American cautionary tale and a most compelling narrative.

The wayward son was Matthew III, the fifth of Phebe and Matthew II's eleven children. He was born at Black Hall in 1688 and from early childhood on was a willful, wild and unruly boy. Headstrong and hard to manage, Matthew III spent his boyhood knocking about in small boats on the Connecticut River and Long Island Sound. He developed a great love for all things nautical and, as he grew into his teen years, resolved to run away to sea. This goal went completely against the wishes of his father, who wanted to keep him on the farm so that he might oversee his son's economic, educational and religious development. However, this regimen of domestic structure did not appeal to the wayward lad.

While his father was attending a session of the General Court, Matthew III hopped aboard a boat bound up the Atlantic coast to New Hampshire's Piscataqua River. In the words of his father, the boy was "willfully forsaking the Duty of his Relations and the means of Grace and ingulphing [*sic*] himself into the temptations of a Wicked World." This was particularly disturbing to the father because the wayward wanderer was a "very weakly lad." Matthew II feared that a sea voyage would be too much for the boy's delicate constitution. Although his subsequent adventures demonstrate that he toughened up quite a bit, his father's fears ultimately came to be realized when the prodigal son finally returned home. The events that transpired between the time he left and his eventual return are full of harrowing hardship, hell-raising and heroism.

At New Hampshire, wayward Matthew III signed on as a crewman before the mast on a merchant vessel bound to the Caribbean. Shortly after they were out in the Atlantic, the ship was buffeted by a tremendous storm. The captain ordered Griswold aloft to clear away a piece of rigging that had broken loose in the storm. Matthew balanced precariously on a length of line, clinging to the yardarm, as the mast pitched wildly from side to side in the tremendous waves. The wayward son lost his grip and plummeted seaward, but at the last moment, he was able to grab a rope and stay his fall enough that he was not badly injured. This near-death experience awakened a spiritual dimension in the young man that hitherto lay dormant. He began to reflect on his defection from his family and began to believe that some agency of divine providence had spared him that he might return home and rectify misdeeds and fulfill his filial obligations.

But a quick round trip back to New England was not to be for the reformed young man. Shortly after his ship arrived in Jamaica, he was captured by a press gang from a British navy man-of-war in a Port Royal alehouse. Impressed into the Royal Navy, he was subjected to a much harsher seagoing life than the one he had experienced aboard the merchantman. Strict discipline, bad food and the constant threat of battle and drowning made for a miserable existence, especially for someone who had experienced the relative freedom of colonial Connecticut in his formative years. Impressed seamen were essentially slaves, doing very hard labor for very low, if any, wages. It was a very trying ordeal that sorely tested young Griswold's newfound religious sensibilities. He served on His Majesty's warship for several months but was able to either desert or was released from his obligation. In the end, he found himself on the beach without a shilling in his pocket.

He soon found a berth on a privateer and once again took to the sea in an armed vessel. This one, however, was a lively fighter, and shortly after joining the crew, Griswold was a participant in several skirmishes with merchant ships and more dangerous naval vessels. During one of these engagements, he was on deck when his friend and shipmate standing next to him was cut to pieces by chain shot, a particularly deadly type of ammunition designed to kill and maim with maximum efficiency. Having escaped death by mere inches, Griswold had another religious epiphany and took firmly to the notion that "God caused him to Reform his Life…He resolved to return as soon as he might be able to his Father's House." He fought in several more violent encounters until he was captured by the French.

He was held as a prisoner on a French naval vessel, kept in irons and given very little in the way of provisions and fresh air. His captors took him to the Bay of Honduras, where he and several others were sold to a party of Spanish Indians under the command of a Spanish army officer. Under almost unendurable conditions, the men were marched coffle style into the jungle. Their hands were tied behind their backs, and they were roped about the neck so they could only proceed single file. In this painful and humiliating fashion, they were paraded some six hundred miles inland and given only a little water "and the cabbage which grows upon trees." To further exacerbate his woes, Griswold contracted "fever and ague" (perhaps malaria), which put him in such a perilous position that he was sure that every painful step would be his last on earth.

According to his father, though, "Yet God marvelously preserved him, while three men much more likely than himself perished upon the road. Upon the End of their journey they were fast chained two by two; and so continued eight months confined, and Languishing in Exquisite Miseries. My Son was visited with the Small Pox while he was in these Wretched Circumstances." While all this was going on, Matthew II was visited by some ministers, who put together some fervent prayers that convinced him that his son was still alive somewhere but that he was in great distress. The clergymen convinced the despairing parent to not give up hope and to continue praying for his son's return and ultimate redemption.

Young Griswold, in the meantime, was having his newfound faith tested by his Spanish captors. They decided that the Roman Catholic Church was his only path to salvation and made concerted efforts to convert him to Catholicism: "Innumerable Endeavors were used in this time by the Father Confessors to persuade them to turn Papist; sometimes promising great rewards, sometimes threatening them with the Mines and Hell." Some of the young prisoner's fellow sufferers did forsake their Protestant roots and convert. They were immediately rewarded by being sent off to the mines, to a life of unimaginable suffering and pain. Griswold held fast to his Puritan beliefs, however, and his steadfastness was unexpectedly rewarded.

A personal and political disagreement arose between the Spanish officer, the governor and the viceroy of the territory where the prisoners were being held. It augured well for our heretofore-luckless hero. The viceroy then propitiously decided that these poor wretches were essentially honest men who had been taken by the French and had no ill will against the Spanish. He then issued a special warrant that they should all be taken, with special care, to the nearest seaport and put on board some Spanish ships and sent to Old Spain, where they would be delivered to the English Counsel and, hopefully, returned to the countries of their origin. The Catholic converts happily shed their new religion and became Protestants again before taking the road to the sea. One of them left behind a wife whom he had married while working in the mines.

The newly freed men were put on Spanish ships and ferried about the Spanish Indies while waiting for the plate fleet to assemble for its voyage back to Spain. Finally, they were put aboard a large galleon and put to sea. Unfortunately for Griswold, while he was on this voyage, he was stricken with a "Dreadful Fever." The ship's doctor offered what ministrations he could but ultimately declared the young man to be past recovery. However, the doctor decided to try one more thing and began to bleed him, a common medical practice of the time. He bled him so much that it seemed all his blood was gone and that the poor youth was, indeed, dead. But when the bleeding stopped, Griswold remarkably sprang back to life and quickly recovered.

This extraordinary occurrence caught the attention of the galleon's captain, who decided the now healthy young man must be blessed in some important way. Since the captain was childless, he offered to adopt Griswold and give him a substantial fortune if he would just embrace the Catholic faith and be baptized into it. While he was contemplating this offer, Griswold injured his leg and came close to losing it. As he once again lay fever stricken and in pain, he had a visitation from the spirit of his mother, long since deceased, who inspired him to forgo the temptations of wealth and ease being offered to him. So he politely declined the captain's kind offer and retained his Protestant faith.

Matthew III landed at Cadiz and from there secured passage to Portugal, where he caught a ship bound for Newfoundland. During that voyage, the injury to his leg healed properly, and he was no longer lame. From Canada, he sailed to Nantucket. While aboard that ship, he was befriended by a man from Boston, who supplied him with food and money. The people of Nantucket were exceedingly kind to him. They entertained him in their homes, fed and clothed him and generally made every amenity available to him. From Nantucket, he made his way to Rhode Island before finally returning to Old Lyme by water, completing an extraordinary adventure, both physical and spiritual.

His father, of course, was ecstatic. Upon his son's return, the Champion noted, "Thus after Four Years were near expired, I received my Son, the truest Penitent that ever my Eyes beheld!" Their joyful reunion was filled with declarations of faith and piety. Old grudges were set aside, forgiveness was requested for past transgressions, vows of faithfulness were renewed and old wrongs were righted. Alas, this state of grace was to be short-lived. Although he arrived home in perfect health, the prodigal son told his father, "My business home was to make my peace with you and to Dy [sic]." Eight weeks after his heartfelt homecoming, Matthew III was dead at age twenty-four. His story might be somewhat apocryphal, but it speaks of a spirit and an era of adventure that still captivates our imaginations today.

The Champion certainly had more than his share of worries due to the adventures and misadventures of his peripatetic son, but he was able to take some solace in the more pious and stable life of his son George. George was born at Black Hall on December 22, 1690. As a child, he was serious and studious. He was never bitten with the wanderlust and remained in the Old Lyme area most of his life. He graduated from Yale College in 1717. His salutatory address in Latin is one of the oldest college-related documents housed in the Yale Library today.

Upon graduation, George chose to follow a spiritual path and became the pastor of the East Lyme Society. He remained in that position until his death in 1761. The Reverend George was a stern, no-nonsense preacher. He was portrayed as a "grave, judicious and godly man; very successful and diligent in his ministry among the people and the Nehantick [sic] Indians." His gravity might have had a dampening effect on the attentiveness that his audiences paid to his sermons. At one point in his ministry, the Nehantics petitioned the church to have him preach to them once every two weeks instead of on a weekly basis.

The Reverend George built a stone church in East Lyme that he dedicated to the grace and glory of God. He passed on his pious spirit to his son Sylvanus Griswold. Following in his father's footsteps, Sylvanus became the pastor of the Agawam, Massachusetts Congregational

Church. He was a fixture in its pulpit for fifty-seven years. He was hired for the then princely sum of $225 per year, plus all the firewood he could burn and forty acres of land. When the church fell on difficult economic times due to the Revolutionary War, Sylvanus graciously agreed to free the congregation from their monetary obligations to him and continued to minister to his flock *gratis*.

Chapter 6

THE GOVERNOR

Matthew IV was the son of John and Hannah Griswold. He was born at Black Hall on March 25, 1714. He was educated at one of the local schools that his father was instrumental in founding at Black Hall in Lyme. His father, known as Judge John, was elected to the Connecticut legislature twenty-eight times and was judge of the quorum for New London County for twenty-nine years. The judge was esteemed for his wisdom and integrity and carried on what was to become a long tradition of public service.

His son, Matthew, did not receive formal, post-secondary education but undertook a rigorous program of self-education specializing in law. In 1742, he was admitted to the New London Bar and opened a lawyer's practice in Lyme. His specialty was estate law and debt collection. His legal career proved to be a stepping-stone to a life of government service that saw him filling a variety of offices at a particularly volatile and significant time in America's history. Matthew IV was a key figure in Connecticut's fight for independence from Great Britain and the formation of the United States.

In spite of his prodigious political accomplishments, much of the popular mythology surrounding this early patriot focuses on his love life. His unsuccessful courtship of a young woman from Durham is an often-told story in family lore. Matthew was quite smitten with this woman and traveled from Lyme to her home and back several times a month. This was not an easy task in the early eighteenth century, when ferry service was sporadic and roads few, far between and poorly maintained. But Matthew steadfastly pursued her hand with a single-minded ardor. The young lady, however, was just stringing him along. She was in love with a local doctor and kept the "farmer Matthew" on the shelf in case that didn't work out. Finally, Matthew issued his ultimatum, demanding that she give him a straight answer once and for all. The coquette hemmed and hawed and pleaded for some more time before issuing her decision. "Madame," grumped Matthew, "you shall have the rest of your life!" And it turns out she did. She wasn't able to land the medical man and spent her years as a spinster.

This experience left the young man a bit love shy—he became very recalcitrant to initiate relationships with women after being burned so badly in an affair of the heart. Fortunately, his cousin Ursula Wolcott had other ideas. She was a strong, forthright, "bright and pretty" woman who became intrigued by all she heard about Matthew's dignity and character. She decided to set her cap for him even before they actually met in person and laid plans to marry him. She convinced herself that she was in love with him and that, with a little encouragement, he could be made to love her, too. But she realized that she would have to take the initiative to fan these amorous sparks into flames.

Ursula arranged to accompany other family members from Windsor for an extended stay at Black Hall. Every now and then, she would ask, "What did you say, Matthew?" Since he rarely said anything to her, he would respond with "Oh, I didn't say anything" or some other noncommittal answer. After several days of this little game, she cornered him on a narrow, winding stairway and asked again, in her brightest, most encouraging and charming voice, "What did you say, Matthew?" Again, the reluctant swain mumbled, "Oh, nothing." Seizing the initiative, Ursula said, "Well, it's about time you did say something! Something like you love me!" Matthew took the hint, and words of love and devotion began to flow from his head and his heart. The couple quickly formed a bond of love and mutual support that would last the rest of their lives. Ursula was unique in that she was the daughter of a governor who became the wife of a governor, the mother of a governor and also a sister and a cousin of a governor.

As Matthew's law practice grew, he became increasingly sought after as a teacher of the law. He attracted many students to Lyme and, in the process, accumulated one of the finest collections of law books in the country. His abilities as a lawyer were rewarded with his appointment as king's attorney for New London County. As such, he represented the interests of England and the colony of Connecticut in courts and civil venues. He was commissioned a captain in the Lyme Train Band, the local militia. In 1751, he was elected to be a deputy for Lyme in the Connecticut General Assembly. This expanded his role in the governance of the colony in conjunction with his duties as king's attorney.

While he was lawyering for the Crown, Matthew became involved in a case that demonstrates how legal ethics were upheld back in his day. He was called on to prosecute a forger and counterfeiter from Killingworth named Abel Buell. Buell must have done something to endear Griswold to him, because he got off quite lightly considering that he was found guilty of what could have been a capital offense. Instead of finding himself at the end of a rope, Buell was sentenced to cropping, branding and a prison term. Griswold arranged to have only a small piece of his ear lopped off, and Buell was able to hide it on his tongue and reattach it. Also, his branding was high enough on his forehead that he was able to cover it with his hair. Matthew also saw to it that the forger could serve his sentence in his hometown of Killingworth. During his confinement, Abel Buell invented a stonecutting machine called a lapidary that was a marked advancement in jewelry making. Perhaps in a show of gratitude for his light sentence, he made Prosecutor Griswold a gold ring set with precious stones.

In his capacity as a deputy, Matthew was selected to be the overseer of the Mohegan Indian Tribe. In the paternalistic relationship between the indigenous people and the colonists of the time, Griswold became responsible for the management of the Indians' property and affairs. He also became involved in the legal dispute known as the Mohegan Case, the first indigenous land rights litigation in the colonies. Its focus was hegemony over land in southeastern Connecticut and the nature of agreements made by John Mason when he decimated the Pequots. The case was of such magnitude that it was brought to the attention of Queen Anne back in Great Britain. She ordered an investigation into the situation, and a Stonington court ruled in favor of the Indians. The colonists complained to the Queen, who looked at the matter again and this time ruled in favor of the colonists. Years of appeals followed. In 1764, Matthew formed a committee to review the situation. He ruled in favor of the colonists, who he believed were entitled to the lands they had worked so hard to improve. He dispatched a friend, William Samuel Johnson, to London to present his case to the Royal Court. The English jurists ruled in the colonists' favor in 1771, putting the matter to rest until the twentieth century and the coming of casinos.

One very interesting task that Matthew Griswold undertook as deputy governor was to chair the committee of inquiry into the mutiny on board the *Minerva*, the first warship commissioned into the Connecticut navy. By happenstance, the *Minerva* was owned by another Griswold, Captain

William, who had left Connecticut to make a small fortune as a sail maker in London before returning to his home state to become a ship owner and merchant. Griswold's ship was fitted out in Rocky Hill, and a crew signed on with the belief that they would be cruising Long Island Sound to prey on British shipping. The *Minerva*'s captain had secret orders to sail for the St. Lawrence River, however, and his secret leaked out. Most of the crew flatly refused to follow orders to sail so far from home, and the ship never made it out of the Connecticut River on its maiden voyage. Matthew's committee punished the two ringleaders of the mutiny and discharged twelve other mutineers. Eventually, the *Minerva* was refitted and saw credible service in the Revolutionary War, capturing several rich British prizes.

Matthew's heyday was a time of social, religious and political upheaval and transformation in Connecticut. He was a member of the First Ecclesiastical Society of Lyme. The region's churches were in the throes of the Great Awakening, a revivalist religious movement that reformed the relationship between the individual and God and questioned the traditional role of the church, its dogma and its rituals. The supporters of these changes were called New Lights, and the traditionalists who liked the status quo were known as Old Lights. Griswold was an avid New Light. Traveling charismatic preachers went from congregation to congregation implanting new ideas and often dividing churchgoers. Some of those divisions took on political and social dimensions in addition to the religious. Griswold served as clerk of the society, and that, coupled with his political activities, set the stage for him to become involved in events that would change the nature of governance in the colony forever. He was also elected to the Council of Assistants to further solidify his political power.

The Stamp Act, passed by the British in 1765, placed high taxes on paper products such as newspapers, pamphlets, legal documents and even playing cards. It was wildly unpopular in the colonies, especially among the New Lights of Connecticut. Griswold was among the opponents of the act who transformed their religious affiliations into a political group called the Sons of Liberty, whose goal was to effect the repeal of the Stamp Act by any means possible. He was among the throng who met with the royal stamp distributor to demand his resignation and the elimination of the policy. All colonial governors were required to take an oath to support the Stamp Act, and Connecticut's governor at the time, Thomas Fitch, did so under duress. Disgusted, Griswold and eight members of the council stormed out of the room to show their contempt for the spineless governor's action. The Stamp Act was repealed in 1766, and the New Lights were seen as part of a victorious movement with growing political clout. Griswold's personal clout increased when he was chosen to be a judge of the Superior Court in 1765.

Political tension between the Old and New Lights continued to fester in the colony. The New Lights, believing eastern Connecticut to be overpopulated, formed an organization called the Susquehanna Company to encourage emigration from Connecticut to Pennsylvania. Pennsylvanians, quite naturally, opposed what they saw as a land grab in their territory and enlisted the Old Lights to fight against the move. The Old Lights feared that the controversy would have negative repercussions in England and that Connecticut's charter might be taken away. As a result, the stage was set for some electoral infighting. Griswold and Declaration of Independence signer Roger Sherman supported the company's land claims, but the Connecticut legislature voted it down. It was finally approved some years later.

But the Pennsylvania brouhaha had unexpected results in the gubernatorial election. Jonathan Trumbull, a supporter of the New Lights, was elected governor. The Old Lights tried to get Thomas Fitch into the deputy governor's seat but were unsuccessful. To everyone's surprise, including his own supporters, Matthew Griswold was elected to the office on the fourth ballot, eclipsing the outspoken New Lighter Eliphalet Dyer, thought to have a lock on the office. Dyer's outspoken radicalness worked against him with many of the moderates, and Griswold became the dark horse winner. He was reelected as deputy governor for several years and was also selected to become the chief justice of the Connecticut Superior Court.

In addition to his political duties, Matthew took a keen interest in education. In 1773, he headed a committee that completely revamped the curriculum at Yale College and introduced innovative pedagogical methods into its classrooms. The college was so appreciative of his efforts that it awarded him the degree of doctor of laws in 1779. By dint of hard work, the autodidact earned the highest of academic honors.

The inevitable military hostilities between Great Britain and its rebellious colonies gave Griswold the opportunity to show what a dedicated patriot he truly was. His support of the colonists' cause encompassed both political and hands-on actions. He became an important member of the Committee of Safety and was a key decision maker, advising the government and military about troop movements and logistics, appointments and commissions of officers, quartermastering, finance, citizen mobilization and political strategies. He was particularly concerned about attacks on colonial shipping by the British navy and raids by British marines on the Connecticut shoreline. During the war, his home at Black Hall was ravaged by British troops on several occasions, prompting Griswold to convince Governor Trumbull to station a permanent platoon of troops in Lyme.

Because of his wartime activities, Matthew was a particular thorn in the sides of the redcoats. They tried unsuccessfully to capture him on at least two occasions. When his wife, Ursula, spotted the English soldiers marching up the lane toward their house, she warned Griswold and hid him in a large sea chest that she covered with a pile of burlap feed sacks. She invited the enemy soldiers in to search the house and served the officers tea while their enlisted men lackadaisically poked around looking for Matthew. They apparently were too lazy to move all the burlap, so they left without their quarry. Ursula breathed a sigh of relief and made herself another cup of tea to celebrate. Family lore suggests that Matthew had a dram of something a bit more potent to acknowledge his escape.

Not long afterward, His Majesty's troops again trudged across Black Hall in search of their avowed enemy. This time, Matthew was just ahead of them. He saw that a neighbor girl, Hetty Marvin, was spreading linens on the lawn to bleach and dry. Without a second to spare, he crawled under the linens and tried not to move or even breathe as the British stood only a few feet away questioning the girl. "Did you see Matthew Griswold pass by here?" grunted a sergeant. "No, I did not see him pass by," the brave girl answered honestly. In fact, he hadn't passed by; he was still right there. Satisfied by the disingenuous answer, the lobsterbacks continued their search while Matthew scurried off to a more secure hiding spot.

In his capacity as a lieutenant of the Train Band, Matthew wound up playing an important role in the world's history of naval warfare. David Bushnell, an eccentric inventor from the west side of the river, was tinkering with the idea of a submersible boat, the *Turtle*, that could stealthily approach enemy vessels under water and attach mines with timers to their hulls to blow them up as they lay at anchor. Several important military and political figures, including Benjamin Franklin, visited Lyme to observe the prototype. Unfortunately, just as Bushnell had almost perfected his prototype, the project ran out of money. Lieutenant Griswold responded by making a non-stop round trip to the War Office in Lebanon and returned with sixty pounds that would ensure that the world's first submarine could be completed. It was less than a success in its attempts to sink enemy warships, but Bushnell's visionary ideas became the fecund font from which sprang all the undersea vessels that followed in the *Turtle*'s wake.

When the Revolutionary War ended, the victorious citizens of Connecticut had become disenchanted with the policies of Governor Trumbull. So in

BY HIS EXCELLENCY

MATTHEW GRISWOLD, Esquire;

Governor, Captain General, and Commander in Chief, in and over the STATE of CONNECTICUT:

A PROCLAMATION.

WHEREAS the Divine Power and Goodness have been wonderfully displayed in the Protection and signal Deliverances granted to the Inhabitants of this Land, from the first Settlement of our Fore-fathers, until the present Time: And marvellous have been the favourable Interpositions of Divine Providence to them and their Posterity in Times of imminent Danger, when repeatedly threatened with Destruction from potent Enemies; until it hath pleased the Most High, who ruleth over the Kingdoms of Men, to give us an equal Rank among the sovereign Nations of the Earth, with the full Enjoyment of our Constitutional Rights, Civil and Religious Liberties and Privileges, in Peace and Tranquillity. And from the same beneficent Hand we at present enjoy the Blessing of Health and Plenty, with innumerable other Favours and Mercies, which call for the highest Praise and Thankfulness to the Great Author of all our Benefits.

I HAVE thought fit, by and with the Advice of the Council, and at the Desire of the Representatives, in General Court assembled, to appoint, and do hereby appoint, THURSDAY, the *Twenty-fourth* Day of *November* next, to be observed as a Day of PUBLICK THANKSGIVING throughout this State: Exhorting Ministers and People, of all Denominations, with Reverence to present their Thank-offerings to the Father of all our Mercies, and to praise him for all the Bounties of his Providence, and richer Blessings of his Grace. In particular to ascribe Thanksgiving and Praise to ALMIGHTY GOD, for the Enjoyment of the Means of Grace; the inestimable Privileges of a preached Gospel; Sabbath and Sanctuary Advantages; for the Continuation of the Blessings of Peace; the general Enjoyment of Health, and plentiful Supplies of the Fruits of the Earth the current Year: And for every Expression of his loving Kindness and tender Mercy. Also at the same Time to implore the Father of Mercies to inspire our national Council, the CONGRESS of these UNITED STATES, with Wisdom and Fidelity equal to the Trust reposed in them: That he may be graciously pleased to confirm and perpetuate the federal Union: That civil Discord and internal Dissentions, or whatever tends to disturb the Happiness, Peace and Prosperity of the Nation, may be prevented: That our civil Administrations may be directed, owned and blessed: That the MOST HIGH would pour out his Spirit in plentiful Effusions upon the Churches and Ministers in this State and Land: That Seminaries of Learning, and other Schools of Instruction, may be happily succeeded: That the People of this State may be smiled upon in their Husbandry, Fishery and Commerce: That the REDEEMER's Kingdom may be advanced abundantly every where; and the World be filled with the glorious Displays of the Divine Perfections, in and through JESUS CHRIST, our LORD and SAVIOUR.

And all servile Labour is forbidden on said Day.

GIVEN under my Hand in the Council Chamber in New-Haven, the seventeenth Day of October, Annoque Domini, 1785.

MATTHEW GRISWOLD.

NEW-HAVEN: Printed by THOMAS and SAMUEL GREEN.

Governor Matthew Griswold's Thanksgiving proclamation. *Courtesy of the Connecticut Historical Society.*

1784, Trumbull chose not to run for reelection. Griswold decided to run for the highest office, but since he was associated with Trumbull, he failed to garner a majority of the vote, much to his chagrin. This put the election in the hands of the General Assembly, which recognized Griswold's service to the colony and chose him to be governor. He was reelected by popular vote in 1785 but lost to Samuel Huntington in 1786.

One of the interesting things that Griswold did while in the governor's office was to promote Thanksgiving as a holiday. Carrying on the Pilgrim tradition, he issued a proclamation that exhorted "Ministers and People of all Denominations, with Reverence to present their Thank-offerings to the Father of all our Mercies, and to Praise him for all the Bounties of his Providence, and richer blessings of his Grace." He customized his urgings to fit the circumstances of the new country when he asked the citizenry to "implore the Father of Mercies to inspire our National Council, the Congress of the United States, with Wisdom and Fidelity equal to the trust reposed in them."

Matthew continued his career of public service even after his gubernatorial defeat. He became president of the Supreme Court of Errors of Connecticut. He was also a strong proponent of the need for a national unity. As such, he became Lyme's delegate to the committee to ratify the U.S. Constitution. He was chosen by his peers to be president of that body and was given the honor of informing Congress that Connecticut had ratified the new government.

Matthew's wife, Ursula, who had cajoled him to speak up and declare his intentions so long ago, died in 1788. Matthew retired from public life and returned to Black Hall to manage his estates and live out his final years on the land he had fought so hard to make free. His last public duty came in 1789, when he was asked to go to New Haven to be a member of the group that assembled to greet George Washington on the first stop of his visit to Connecticut. Griswold died in 1799, leaving a legacy of service to Connecticut that is one of the hallmarks of its eighteenth-century history. That legacy included a son who was to also become a governor of Connecticut.

Chapter 7

THE BIG STICK FEDERALIST

That son, Roger Griswold, apparently inherited the pugnacious streak exhibited by the Champion. Roger was born at Black Hall on May 25, 1762. He was the son of Governor Matthew Griswold and the grandson of Roger Wolcott, also a governor. This political pedigree set him on a path to practicing law and then on to a variety of public offices. His career was highlighted by a boys-will-be-boys-even-when-they-are-men fracas on the floor of Congress. That rather raucous encounter serves as a seminal symbol of the divisions between political parties that continue to cause legislative gridlock and mudslinging unpleasantness in our present national legislative arena.

Roger matriculated at Yale University at the age of fourteen. He graduated in 1780 and proceeded to take up the study of law under the tutelage of his father. He was admitted to the Connecticut Bar at the age of twenty-one and began a stellar career in the legal world. According to Frederick Calvin Norton's *The Governors of Connecticut*, "Great success was his from the first, and few men in the state ever acquired a greater reputation at the bar than Roger Griswold." His law office in Norwich drew clients from around the state, and his reputation as brilliant a litigator garnered notice from those within his family's political network and beyond.

After a decade of practicing law in what has come to be known as the Rose City, he returned home to Old Lyme and campaigned for national office. He became a staunch member of the Federalist Party and was elected to the U.S. House of Representatives in 1795. He was reelected five times

Governor Roger Griswold's house, circa 1840. *Courtesy of the Connecticut Historical Society.*

and served admirably. Roger's "ability and profound judgment placed him in the front ranks of congressmen," according to contemporary sources.

His period of congressional service spanned a key era of growth and development of the national government. He was in office for part of Washington's administration, all of John Adams's and some of Thomas Jefferson's. He helped to frame the nature and culture of Congress and had input in defining the relationships between the legislative, executive and judicial branches of government. He was an undisputed leader of his party and "was distinguished for his powerful talents in debate, and the independence and decision of his conduct." It was some of that conduct that got him into hot water on the floor of the House. He also held important committee assignments, including the Committee on Revisions and Unfinished Business and the House Ways and Means Committee.

Roger was highly esteemed by his peers—at least the ones who agreed with his political positions. According to Norton, "In personal appearance he was a very handsome man, with large flashing eyes, a commanding figure, and majestic mien. He seemed by outward presence born to rule." Connecticut's chief justice Waite wrote of him, "In all positions he proved himself a born master of men. Few have been more universally esteemed and loved. He lived in a critical and eventful time in our existence; and preeminently acted well his part, deserving and receiving the highest honors his native state could bestow on him." As we shall see, a certain congressman from Vermont did not hold Griswold in quite so high a level of esteem.

While Roger was serving in Congress, President John Adams sought him out to serve as the secretary of war. Roger declined the request. In 1803, Roger, along with several other New England Federalists, proposed that the Northeast secede from the Union in opposition to the growing power of Jeffersonian Democrats after the Louisiana Purchase. After his terms in Congress were over, Roger returned to Connecticut, where he became a Superior Court judge. He was a presidential elector on the unsuccessful Pinckney and King ticket and served as lieutenant governor of Connecticut from 1809 to 1811. He received a doctor of laws degree from Harvard University in 1811 and another one from Yale in 1812. He was elected governor of Connecticut in 1811 and was reelected in 1812, serving at a time when the nation was starkly divided over the issues surrounding the War of 1812.

Roger was a hard-line opponent of "Mr. Madison's War." He saw it as an economic disaster for the Northeast, which was economically dependent on shipping and shipbuilding. The Embargo Act devastated the shipping business in New England for decades. Ships built by the Griswold family were outfitted as privateers to raid British vessels. One of their ships, the *Black Prince*, an eighteen-gunner fitted out as a privateer, was destroyed by the Royal Navy when twenty-eight American ships were burned during the infamous Raid on Essex, or the Battle of Essex, as some contemporary historians style it. The *Black Prince* was towed downriver by British sailors under the command of Lieutenant Coote and burned at the mouth of the river.

President Madison requested that Governor Griswold provide four companies of Connecticut troops to serve with the U.S. Army. Roger declined to do so, saying that they were not necessary to deter an invasion of Connecticut. But the British invasion came closer to Connecticut than Roger anticipated, as the mouth of the Connecticut River was constantly being patrolled by English warships. The residents of Black Hall, along with other Lyme residents, kept a close lookout at several strategic sites in town, including Watch Rock. Some makeshift defenses were constructed but never used. After the war, townsfolk would find the odd cannonball and other discarded munitions left over from the era. Some field guns were positioned to fire on the enemy ships, but since the British forces were overwhelmingly superior, it was decided that they would be used only if the English mounted a direct attack on the town. Since that never occurred, it is commonly believed that no shots were fired in anger from Lyme. But recent historical revisions and research indicate that the Lyme cannon might have seen some use.

The only direct attack on Lyme occurred in conjunction with the Raid on/Battle of Essex. On April 8, 1814, the British sent three barges and two launches manned by 136 seamen up the river to burn American ships. On their way back downstream, they stopped and burned several vessels at Brockway's Ferry on the Lyme side of the river. They then rowed back to their mother ships anchored in Long Island Sound, having enjoyed enough "incendiary sport," as it was called at the time. One of the Griswold brothers, Charles, also a lawyer, joined a group of citizens at Higgins Wharf to observe the fiery action in Essex. He later watched the British slip downstream from the beach at Black Hall. In a letter to his cousin Ebenezer Lane, he described the day's action and its devastating effects on the American vessels: "Although there was a large collection of people on both sides of the river, yet there was no efficient force at all...a mere multitude without order, discipline or a head. Of courage and zeal there was sufficient, but no means of employing them to advantage and effect. I was on the beach when the boats rowed out of the river and saw their blue lights on the dark water." He estimated the damage to be between $100,000 and $150,000, an enormous sum at the time. Charles Griswold concluded that the raid could not have been prevented and that no one should be held financially or legally accountable for the damage and losses.

Roger's opposition to the war notwithstanding, it is his role in one of the seamiest episodes in the history of the early U.S. Congress for which he will long be remembered. It is interesting to note that many of the issues that led up to his famous (or infamous) confrontation with Matthew Lyon are still being debated today. Just as our country is still struggling with immigration, class warfare and legislative procedures and process, so, too, did it in Roger's time. His brawl with Lyon was a fight between men, but it was also the result of conflict between political, social and cultural ideologies and identities. It pitted native born against foreign born, aristocrat against "a man of the people" and the interests of the few against those of the many. It was one of the defining events in the development of the factional nature of democracy and the political climate that infuses our country today.

Lyon was born into poverty in Dublin, Ireland, in 1749. He was apprenticed to a printer and learned that trade, which served him well throughout his life. He secured passage aboard a ship to Connecticut as a redemptioner—an emigrant whose passage is paid for in exchange for his agreement to work as a bond servant for a specified period of time. Lyon worked on a farm in Woodbury, Connecticut, to pay off his indenture and continued to educate himself, especially in the areas of law and politics. After his debt was paid, he moved to Wallingford, Vermont, where he put together a band of militia to serve in the Revolutionary War. He was eventually commissioned a second lieutenant in the outfit that became the legendary Green Mountain Boys.

It was during the war that the seeds of the fight with Griswold were sown. Lyon was in charge of a company of men during an obscure encounter near the Canada-Vermont border. His men mutinied, and Lyon was held at fault and drummed out of the army. Rumor had it that he was forced to wear a wooden sword as a symbol of his cowardice and mismanagement of his troops. He was later exonerated and welcomed back into the army at a rank above his old one. But his reputation had been tarnished and his courage called into question, something that his political adversaries, including Roger Griswold, were not liable to forget very quickly. After the war, he returned to Vermont, where he established a printing business and newspaper and was elected to the state legislature and, eventually, the House of Representatives.

The fight began when several members of the House gathered around a fireplace, chatting and informally counting votes on an upcoming bill. Lyon turned to Griswold and accused him of enriching himself at the expense of their constituents. He said that since he had a large printing company, he would go after Griswold in the public eye and call him out for the blue-blooded elitist that he was. Griswold responded that if Lyon planned on coming to Connecticut, he better bring his wooden sword with him because he was going to need it. Lyon then squeezed a significant amount of tobacco juice from the chaw he had wadded in his cheek and spat it into Roger's face! Griswold produced a linen handkerchief; wiped the spittle from his brow, nose and cheeks; and quietly left the room.

The Federalist colleagues of Griswold immediately responded by introducing a measure that would have expelled Lyon from the House. On February 14, the measure passed by a margin of 52 to 44. However, since it was not the two-thirds majority necessary in such situations, Lyons remained in Congress. That evening, Roger purchased a stout, hickory walking stick. He spent the night brooding and stewing over his insulted honor. At some point, he decided that since Lyon had not been removed from the House, he would have to secure revenge by other means.

The following day, Roger brought his newly acquired cudgel with him to Congress. Without warning, he walked over to Lyon, declared that he was a scoundrel and began bashing him soundly about the head and shoulders. He managed to land several punishing blows before Lyon was able to make his way to the fireplace and grab a pair of tongs with which to defend himself. Roger tripped Lyon and sent him sprawling. He wrested the tongs from the Vermont Republican and landed a few more whacks to his face before several astonished legislators were able to subdue him.

Roger tried to rationalize his behavior by stating that being spat on was such an affront to his honor that it absolutely had to be appeased. He felt that Lyon did the spitting because he was, essentially, foreign-born rabble, not fit to consort with gentlemen. Lyon wound up getting reelected to Congress while he was in jail for violating the Alien and Sedition Act, which forbade criticizing the government or its elected officials in print. He moved to Kentucky and was elected to Congress from that state. He wound up being the factor to the Cherokee Nation in the Arkansas territory.

The confrontation was the source of endless jokes and cartoons. The humor of the day is hard to understand now, but Griswold's attack was compared to Heracles slaying the Nemean Lion. Lyon's expectoration on Griswold was likened to Socrates's wife dumping a chamber pot on his head. Alluding to Cervantes, Griswold was dubbed the "Knight of the Rheum-full Countenance." The distinctions between Griswold's native birth and Lyon's Irish one inspired such couplets as "A Yankee young dog! To strike a bold Paddy / A man old enough to be his grand-daddy" and "When lo! The fierce Yankee flew into a passion / And gave the bog-trotter a notable thrashing."

Griswold felt completely justified in his actions. In a letter to his wife, he notes, "The newspaper squibs that have and will appear on the occasion are of no consequences—they may tell lies as usual, but they cannot take off the beating." In the same letter, he self-righteously defends his actions: "I did not feel willing to return to Connecticut after the insult I received in so public a manner, without taking satisfaction…the events have perfectly justified the measure. And though my enemies may condemn the harshness of the remedy, yet my friends will approve of it."

Roger, his insult having been satisfied, returned to Connecticut to serve as a jurist and governor. Afflicted with a worsening heart condition, he moved to Norwich to be near his physician, Dr. Tracy. It was hoped that the change of air would help, but his health continued to worsen. He died while still in the governor's office on October 25, 1812. He was only fifty years old when his political career came to an untimely end.

Roger was eulogized eloquently and euphorically by many of his family members, colleagues and constituents. Inscribed on a family monument near Black Hall is the following:

> *He was respected in the university as an elegant classical scholar; quick discernment, sound reasoning, legal science and manly eloquence raised him to the first eminence at the bar. Distinguished in the national councils among the illustrious statesmen of his age* [and] *revered for his inflexible integrity and pre-eminent talents, his political course was highly honorable...His fame and honor were the first rewards of noble action, and a life devoted to his country...His memory is embalmed in the hearts of surviving relatives, and of a grateful people. When his monument shall have decayed, his name will be enrolled with honor among the great, the wise and the good.*

The summer after Roger died, a landing party from the British fleet that was blockading Long Island Sound under the command of Sir Thomas Hardy landed at Black Hall and amused themselves on the beach. They visited Roger's widow, Fanny Rogers Griswold, and asked for some refreshments. They apparently behaved quite civilly and went back to their ships without incident. Fanny remained a widow devoted to the memory of her husband. She lived to be ninety-seven, having been alive for the Revolutionary War, the War of 1812 and the Civil War.

Fanny and Roger had nine children. Several of the males became sea captains of international repute, often working for the NL&G Griswold Company. Among these was the eldest son, Augustus Henry Griswold, who was one of the pioneers of the transatlantic packet trade. In 1816, Augustus took command of the Connecticut River–built brig *Cornelia*. He also skippered the *Comet* in the Savannah-to-New York cotton trade. He finished his career with his cousin John's Black X Line, where he commanded the *Cincinnatus*, the *Acasta*, the *Cambria* and the *Samuel Robertson*, carrying passengers between New York and London. His brother William Frederick Griswold would also become a shipmaster, spending years at sea as a captain and navigator in the China trade. Robert Harper Griswold also had a notable career as a ship's captain.

Another son, Colonel Charles Chandler Griswold (he was given the title for his service to his father as a governor's aide), was a Yale-educated lawyer. On a trip to England, he learned that the church on Meeting House Hill in Old Lyme had burned down and then made painstaking designs from churches near London that were finalized by famous architect Christopher

Wren. The designs were incorporated into the new church when it was built in 1817. The colonel was also responsible for planting the rows of elm trees that formed a natural archway down the lane to Black Hall. Unfortunately, the trees fell victim to Dutch elm disease, but the lane remains much as it did when Roger walked down it a couple centuries ago.

Chapter 8

PIRATE TREASURE AND TORRID ROMANCE

Deacon John Griswold was born at Black Hall in April 1752. He was a man noted for his piety, but his true fame was the result of his great size and prodigious strength. Deacon John was notoriously hard on his horses. Once, he apparently knocked one cold with a blow of his ham-sized fist. What the horse did to provoke such a reaction was not recorded. Another poor equine met even a crueler fate at the hands, or rather the posterior, of the deacon when the latter's hefty hams broke the back of the sorry steed. John married a member of the Diodati family, an Italian aristocracy of long and noble lineage. He and his wife had seven children. It is the romantic tale inspired by his daughter Sarah that serves to link the Griswolds of Black Hall with the Gardiner family of a unique and fabled New York island.

Gardiner's Island lies about ten miles south of Griswold Point off the coast of Long Island. It is named for Lion Gardiner, the military engineer who established a fort at the mouth of the Connecticut River in 1636. Gardiner was instrumental in forcing the Dutch to leave the Connecticut River Valley. He also played a key role in the winning of the Pequot War, which gave the English permanent control of the river and its surrounding territory. His eponymous island was granted to him by King Charles I in 1639 and has remained a family fiefdom for almost four hundred years (although its legal status will permanently change in 2035). Gardiner originally called the island the Isle of Wight because it reminded him of that place back in England. This was an apt name considering its proximity to Lyme, Connecticut.

Not only did Gardiner have claim to the island by right of royal charter, but he also purchased it from the Montuakett Indians for the price of a large black dog, some Dutch blankets and a small quantity of gunpowder and ammunition. The native people called the island *Manchonake*, which chillingly translates to "The Place Where Many Have Died." This unfortunate name is a reference to the fatal epidemics that swept across the island periodically. The Montauketts were inclined to give Gardiner a good real estate deal because they were very grateful for his help in subduing the Pequots, who had terrorized the indigenous communities up and down the Connecticut River and along the Connecticut and Rhode Island coasts. The Pequots had been booted out of what became New York State by the Iroquois Confederation and then began terrorizing the river and sound. The English finally launched a military campaign that all but exterminated them. Lion Gardiner supplied troops, armaments and logistical support to this effort.

Wyandanch, the sachem of the Montauketts, watched the hostilities between the English and the Pequots from across the sound with a wary eye. His natural allegiance would be with the Pequots, but Lion Gardiner was a staunch supporter of his tribe. Also, the chief realized that eventually the superior English firepower would win the day, so he pledged his support and, eventually, his island to Gardiner. Once hostilities ended, Gardiner retired to his insular fiefdom and went about the business of siring a family that would rule the island as their private demesne for centuries. Interestingly, his daughter was caught up in one of the first witchcraft intrigues in New York, much like Matthew Griswold I's wife. There is a lasting belief that she was killed by the witch whom she accused of practicing the black arts.

The Gardiners established a plantation on the island that flourished as succeeding generations husbanded and improved the property. It was not always easy, however. On more than one occasion, Spanish pirates landed and pillaged the land and buildings. In one instance, a Gardiner progeny had his hand lopped off by a Spanish sword. However, the family was, for the most part, successful in fending off these piratical assaults. By the eighteenth century, Spanish sea power was on the wane. Assaults by marauding bands of Spaniards no longer posed a threat to the well-being of the Gardiner family.

But that is not to say that the island became pirate free. The Spanish buccaneers were replaced by boatloads of English corsairs, the most famous being the notorious Captain William Kidd. Kidd made an arrangement with the Gardiner who was lord of the manor at the time of his landing to stash a fortune in stolen booty on the shores of Gardiner's Island. The

Old boats washed ashore served as the perfect setting in which to play pirate. *Griswold family archives.*

English buccaneer's crew unloaded chests of gold doubloons, bars of silver, damask tapestries, emeralds, rubies and diamonds. Kidd gave Gardiner's wife a bolt of gold cloth to commemorate the event. Lord of the Manor Gardiner was able to secret a large diamond in a well bucket, unbeknownst to the sea raider. Kidd sailed off to ultimately meet his fate on the gallows of London Dock, where his body was left to rot in chains as a *memento mori* and a warning to seafarers to keep their activities on the up and up.

This doubly purloined jewel plays an interesting role in the history of Griswold Point. At the very beginning of the nineteenth century, John Gardiner, the seventh lord of the manor of Gardiner's Island, was an unlikely candidate for a passionate love affair. He was a quiet, reserved, Princeton-educated scholar. A devoted naturalist and an early anthropologist, he lived a quiet life on his baronial estate. Among his many projects and interests was the compilation of a dictionary of the Montaukett language, on which he worked diligently, realizing that the culture of the indigenous people was in danger of fading out of people's memory. It was a quirk of nature and the weather that interrupted his idyllic days as a bachelor.

A sailing party from Old Lyme, organized by Sarah Griswold, spent one summer afternoon becalmed within view of Gardiner's island fiefdom. When the breeze finally picked up, it did so with gusto. It went from flat calm to a full gale in a matter of minutes. The boaters made for the nearest safe haven, which was Gardiner's Island. They put into a sheltered cove and ran to the manor house, where the drenched and shaken sailors were taken in by the housekeeper and given dry clothing and a glass of spirits to calm their nerves.

As related by the author of *The History of the City of New York*, "Presently the handsome young lord [Gardiner] put in his appearance, and when he learned who his visitors were, he extended cordial hospitalities. An elaborate supper was served and music and dancing followed. The next morning the delighted refugees bid their charming host adieu." Although she sailed away from his island, Sarah had found a special place in John Gardiner's mind and heart.

He, in fact, had fallen madly in love with Sarah Griswold, a Black Hall beauty with a fiery spirit. Sarah was the granddaughter of Governor Matthew and the sister of John and Charles Griswold, owners of the Black X Line. It cannot be determined whether their marriage was an elopement or not, but "the scion of Gardiner Manor came courting at Black Hall in a splendid barge, well-manned by crewmen in livery. John Gardiner leapt out on the beach so impatiently to salute his lady-love, Mistress Sarah Griswold, that he stained his fine, top-boots in a salt ripple." Family lore has it that he presented her with Captain Kidd's diamond to seal their troth. They were married on March 4, 1803, and settled on the island where Sarah had been blown by the winds of destiny, thus uniting two of the earliest English families in the Connecticut–New York area.

The Diodati connection, however, resulted in a love story that had a much sadder, more ignominious ending. The villain was Diodate Griswold. He, like many family members, went to Yale. He graduated, although he was known for his extravagant wardrobe rather than his scholarship. His outward finery belied many inner weaknesses. He was given to conviviality and was not a prudent money manager. At one point, several tailors had him arrested for non-payment of debts on his fancy clothes. Such was his character when he met and fell in love with Sarah Colt, a beautiful, spritely woman from a respectable Hartford family.

Sadly, Sarah, the object of Diodate's love and devotion, was deeply in love with another fellow but was too amenable to Griswold's entreaties of ardor and passion. She became engaged to her favorite and hoped Diodate would simply go away. But he didn't. Shortly before their scheduled marriage, Sarah's beloved made a business trip to New York State and fell desperately ill with a fever, which put him into a coma. He regained consciousness but suffered from amnesia and couldn't recall who he was or where he was from.

The Black X Line ship *Palestine* with its topsails furled. *Griswold family archives.*

This seventeenth-century bench has the story of a love affair intricately carved into it. *Photo by Ray Guasp.*

Naturally, Sarah was greatly concerned, but she was unsure as to his exact whereabouts and couldn't do anything to contact him.

Seizing his chance, Diodate began to poison Sarah's mind against her beloved. He concocted stories of abandonment and alienated affections. He convinced Sarah that her paramour had run off with a woman of easy virtue and that he stood steadfast and ready to take his place in her life and bring her eternal happiness. Much to her ultimate chagrin, Sarah relented and hastily agreed to marry Diodate. She soon found out that eternal happiness was not to be found with such a carousing dandy, so she resigned herself to a life of sadness and economic uncertainty.

To make matters worse for her, the fiancé recovered his memory and returned to Hartford to claim his bride. It was all downhill from there. Sarah separated from Diodate and obtained a divorce, which was virtually unheard of at the time. Eventually, after being abandoned by her true love, she moved out of state and lived a lonely life. Diodate continued his improvident ways until he found himself in financial, mental and physical ruin. The one-time fashion plate ended his days in a Hartford insane asylum. His fate was brought on by a surfeit of high living and low loving.

Chapter 9
JAMES THE AESTHETE

A descendant of Matthew Griswold has traced family connections, by birth or marriage, to 43 judges of the high courts and 16 governors of the states, one of the last of whom is currently the President of the United States." This was written as a prelude to the obituary sketch of James Griswold, which turned out to be an amazing piece of damnation by faint praise. It turns out that James's distinguished heritage was too much for him to bear. He feared he could never live up to the expectations that such an industrious family would have for him. Instead, it seems that James chose a course of genteel slacking that was interestingly summarized in an "obituary sketch" in the proceedings of the Connecticut Supreme Court. The writer of the obituary noted:

> With such an ancestry and family connections as James Griswold had, another man, taking for his motto "noblesse oblige," might have been ambitious to reach the heights of his profession and of political life. No one who know him could doubt that he possessed the industry, calm dispassionate judgment, the clear insight, bright intellect, thorough knowledge of the law, and the ready and witty use of the best language to convey his ideas—in brief, the thoroughly furnished "legal mind," which might have brought him to distinguished success. But with his sensitiveness, modesty, and habit of undervaluing himself, his ancestral honor depressed, rather than stimulated him. This in a great degree accounts for the undemonstrative and quiet course which he pursued through his life. Not attempting to do great things,

he filled so full of duty and daily kindness the narrower range which he had laid out for himself, that he is missed and mourned in his own sphere as few men in any sphere have the privilege to be. He had time for much reading in many lines of thought, for the study and practice of music of the highest class, and for the use of his keen wit, gentle humor and knowledge of books, and of colonial and contemporary history, and wide practical information, in intercourse with the few friends who had the privilege of his intimate acquaintance.

But there was more to the story of James than this testament to his lack of ambition would indicate. He was born on February 8, 1828, the son of Colonel Charles Griswold and the grandson of Governor Roger Griswold. He graduated from Yale in 1848, was admitted to the bar in 1856 and began practicing law in Old Lyme soon thereafter. It was believed that there was something in the atmosphere and associations of that quaint community that produced much more than its share of great lawyers and judges. Into this environment, "where the very air is laden with the memories of the historic past," James attempted to carry on the distinguished legal traditions of his family and fellow townsmen.

According to Augustus Brandagee, Esquire, a contemporary of his:

James had the gift of a charming personality. He was of medium height, graceful figure, light wavy hair, blue eyes, and an address at once reserved and persuasive, which bespoke confidence and trust at first sight. His conversation was replete with a quaint humor which gave an added charm to the vigorous Anglo-Saxon in which he clothed his thought. He had a certain air of high breeding about him, easily distinguishable, but difficult to describe...he was neither by temperament nor taste fitted for the stormy arena of conflict in the courts—those battles of the bar where blows are given and received, and where all the energies of the mind and body must be marshaled whether for assault, for parry or for defense. He was by nature modest and undemonstrative, and his sensitive soul shrank from the "sound of the trumpets, the thunder of the trumpets and the shoutings." His tastes were cultivated and refined. He loved music and books, pictures and fields, trees and flowers and above all his family and friends. He was at one with nature and held with her congenial converse—whether in the sweet scented woods, or amid the daisies and lilies of the field, or along the banks of the silent river, ever flowing past his door to the bosom of the ocean, or beneath the unspeaking heavens spangled with stars. He was fond of reading, and

Artist Scott Kahn painted the Colonel Charles Chandler Griswold House. He named the painting *Homage to America*. *Photo by Scott Kahn.*

his memory was stored with the choicest productions of both English and classical literature. And from this source, aided by a sparkling originality of his own, he drew forth treasures new and old, which gave a piquant zest to his conversation and made him a most delightful companion.

Nor was he a mere idle dreamer of dreams. To his sweet and gentle nature were added some of those masterful gifts and qualities by which leadership amongst men is compelled. His mind was vigorous, clear, penetrating and judicial. He easily mastered the learning of the law, and explored its primal principals to their deep foundation. He knew when and how to insist on their deep application in all their rigor and when to adapt their flexible conditions to the ever varying requirements of social life and human affairs.

He was endowed with that supreme gift of common sense, which has an intuitive perception of the relations of things, which distinguishes between the sham and the real, the false and the true, and which is greater than genius because it is more useful. I was for the possession of this rare faculty, and the absolute probity of his character, that is came to pass that he was more frequently selected by the judges and by his brethren for the hearing of those causes which are tried out of court, than any other member of the bar.

His temper, his tastes, his leisure, his patience, his impartiality, his supreme love of justice and truth, all conspired to make him a model arbitrator, committee or referee. And in the decision of the many important questions which came before these tribunals, his judgment was rarely at fault and seldom overruled.

With such qualities of mind and heart he soon came to be all to all his neighbors and townsfolk, not only their oracle, but their guide, their counselor and friend. He was the composer of strife and the promoter of peace to the entire community in which he lived. His sense of honor was a lofty as any knight templar who ever set a lance in rest; his word when once passed was as a sacrament; to him a stain was like a wound; his measure of courtesy to rich and poor alike was noblesse oblige. He had an instinctive aversion to the whole brood of shams, hypocrasies [sic], subterfuges and lies.

Chapter 10

NO LOSS, GREAT GAIN

Nathaniel Lynde Griswold and George Griswold began building ships on the Connecticut River in the late eighteenth century. Some of their vessels were attacked and destroyed by the British during the War of 1812. In 1796, when they were still young men, they removed themselves from Old Lyme to New York, where they set up shop in a former flour store on Front Street and created a shipping business that became a legendary commercial enterprise. The New York legislature passed a law in 1833 that required a business to be named for the original founders only if the original founders or their heirs still controlled it. As of the late 1860s, the N.L. & G. Griswold (N.L. & G.G.) Company fit those criteria. Since the products they shipped were stamped with "N.L. & G.G.," wags around the country—and the world, for that matter—insisted that they stood for "No Loss, Great Gain." The brothers from Lyme ruled over a very successful enterprise that spanned the globe and were instrumental in building and sailing some of the greatest ships in the history of the U.S. Merchant Marines.

According to *The Old Merchants of New York*, by Walter Barret, Nathaniel and George "were grand old fellows…tall, imposing…both brothers were men that you would take a second look at." It should be noted that others described them as "hatchet-faced New Englanders." Nathaniel bucked the fashion sense of his day and preferred slouch hats to the toppers sported by most merchants. In 1803, they moved their business to South Street into a "new, rough granite building…There is a fitness in things, and the solid stone was just the building for two such men as Nathaniel and George

The N.L. & G. Griswold clipper ship *Panama* was one of several with that name. *Griswold family archives.*

Griswold…Their signature was as bold as their firm, always highlighted by a good old-fashioned flourish underneath it." Barret is effusive in his praise of the brothers: "These Griswolds sprang from a grand old race. They were Connecticut born at Old Lyme on the Connecticut River. Their ancestor, George, was born in 1692, and 102 years later his boys left Old Lyme for a larger port, at which they were destined in after years to become eminent merchants."

At the outset of their business, they shipped flour to the West Indies and, in return, imported large quantities of sugar and rum, staples of the plantation economy at the time. Since the seventeenth century, a symbiotic relationship existed between the Northeast and the Caribbean. With the need for food and building materials on the islands and the East Coast's insatiable thirst for rum and the Anglophilic habit of sugaring tea, it proved to be a very lucrative trade that was carried on for centuries. The dark underside of the trade, though, was that it was the lifeblood of the plantation culture on the islands and, as a result, depended on slavery for its existence. The Griswolds got their start in the West Indies trade but soon set their sights on farther horizons.

It was their expansion into the China trade that truly made their fortune. It became the mainstay of their enterprise for years, and they designed and built ships expressly for that trade. They owned a succession of ships named *Panama* that served as the workhorses of their fleet. As each one was worn out with hard service, a larger one was built and commissioned to take its place. The first was 465 tons burden, the second 650 tons and the third a whopping 1,170 tons. Between them, they made dozens of voyages between New York and Canton, each one usually more profitable than the last. The Griswolds took advantage of lenient government policies regarding duties on tea to leverage a large share of the market of that hot beverage that nineteenth-century Americans found irresistible.

As Barret notes, "I do not suppose that there is a country store, however insignificant, in the entire United States that has not seen a large or small package of tea marked 'Ship Panama' and 'N.L & G.G.' stamped upon it. Millions and millions of packages must have been imported from the first to the last." Since speed was essential in terms of getting the first cuttings of the savory leaf to market, each Griswold ship was faster than the last, and their greater carrying capacities naturally resulted in more lucrative profits. Since tea was a major driving force in the development of the fledgling American economy, it can truthfully be said that the Griswold brothers helped build the country in a very palpable way. There also can be little doubt that Griswold ships occasionally carried cargoes of opium and silks, but tea was their primary stock in trade.

Like others in the shipping business at the time, the Griswolds not only owned their own ships but also built, brokered, chartered and freighted ships owned by others. Griswold-built ships were in great demand because they not only eschewed frills and fancy work but were also always built of the "best material...upper works made of all live oak, locust and cedar, fastened with wrought copper; duck and cordage of the first quality; completely found in sails, rigging and furniture, and needing nothing whatever. They built their ships strong and good in those days. There was less fancy work but all was solid, seaworthy and substantial." The Griswold house flag, a blue-and-white checkerboard with five blocks in each horizontal row, flew proudly from some of the finest ships that plied the world's oceans during the nineteenth century.

Seaworthiness was of particular importance at the time because many merchants and ship owners were their own insurers. Due to the decades-long slump in shipping that resulted from the War of 1812, there was not much capital in New York and other eastern ports. Shippers like the Griswolds took enormous risks with each voyage. A ship that never returned to port was a loss not only in terms of its crew and officers but also as a financial loss that could devastate the fortunes of stakeholders in the voyage. Liberal government policies regarding the duties on tea enabled the brothers to get credit arrangements that paid for most of the trip in advance and provided specie to trade for tea in China. But in order to turn a profit, the ship still had to return safely to New York.

The Griswolds were on the cutting edge of the development of clipper ships. As the demand for speedy passages increased, they responded by commissioning some of the fastest, most beautiful clipper ships ever to grace the oceans. The *Challenge* was a classic example of this genre of sailing vessels, the epitome of marine architecture and engineering. Built in 1851 by the famous Webb Yard of New York for the California gold rush trade, the *Challenge* is immortalized in the stories of its maiden voyage around Cape Horn. The Griswolds offered Captain "Bully" Waterman a $10,000 bonus if he could take the ship from New York to San Francisco in ninety days or less. Waterman found himself in command of a surly and mutinous crew of greenhorns. The desertions of seamen for the California gold fields made competent sailors hard to find. His first major problem was with the first mate, whom he had to strip of his duties and remove from the ship. His replacement proved to be a disaster.

Despite an inadequate crew, Waterman sailed the speedy clipper hard around the horn. However, his new first mate revealed himself to be a sadistic brute, cruelly killing a sailor by bashing in his head. Waterman had to resort to the use of pistols to keep his mutinous crew from wreaking revenge on his first officer. The *Challenge* arrived in San Francisco 108 days after leaving New York, so Waterman did not earn the Griswolds' incentive bonus. Upon reaching port, he was arrested by U.S. marshals and taken into custody for his own protection, lest disgruntled crewmen do him harm. His first mate was charged with murder. Waterman was never prosecuted and gave up the sea to become a successful California farmer. His first mate was convicted but never punished.

George Griswold has become a unique figure in American clipper ship history—not through his acumen as a ship owner or his ability to lash a recalcitrant crew around Cape Horn but because he had a clipper ship named for him. On its most memorable voyage, the *George Griswold* had fitted out for New York with a cargo of relief supplies for the starving poor of Great Britain. It was a very humanitarian effort by the United States, a country that was struggling with civil war. The ulterior motive was to help the English, whose livelihood had been affected by the war, and to enlist their sympathies in the Union cause. The bread and medicine was distributed by none other than Henry Beecher Ward, a star preacher at the time and one of the most famous men in America.

In the midst of the return trip from this very altruistic voyage, the *Griswold* was captured by the Confederate raider *Georgia*. According to *Recollections of a Rebel Reefer*, the journal of a sailor on the *Georgia*, he and his crew captured a "splendid big clipper ship" that almost out-ran the steam-powered raider after setting its "kites and studding sails." A few shots across *Griswold*'s bow, however, brought it to, and it was boarded by the Rebels. The sailor noted, "The prize proved to be the clipper ship *George Griswold* of New York, manned by a negro crew with the exception of her captain and mates." There was some contention as to whether the capture had taken place in neutral Brazilian waters. The upshot was that the cargo proved to be neutral, so the Confederate captain bonded the *Griswold* for $100,000 and sent it on its way. This didn't sit well with the Rebel crew members, however, who were still incensed at the disparaging remarks about the South made in England upon the distribution of the relief bread.

The Griswold brothers indelibly stamped their imprimatur on the golden age of sail. From the China trade to the clippers, they spirited the young nation's trade and unfurled its flag in the far corners of the globe. But shipping wasn't their only source of income. Nathaniel invented a dredging machine that he used to clean out the Albany basin on the Hudson River and several slips on the New York docks. He then patented his machine and manufactured several, sending them up and down the eastern seaboard to clear channels and create mooring slips. They also leased many docks in New York and made a tidy profit collecting the wharf fees on them.

Nathaniel was a somewhat shy and retiring fellow and had no interest in anyone's business other than his own. George, on the other hand, was the consummate corporate board member. As a young man, he was elected to the board of the Columbia Insurance Company. He went on to become a director of a multitude of companies and societies, including the Bank of America and the Bank of the United States. He was heavily involved in land speculation and bought up large tracts of Brooklyn. He also had a hand in several gold mines, primarily in North Carolina, before the California strike. He was a director of the humane society and was noted for his altruistic endeavors for the benefit of the poor.

George also had a political bent. He worked tirelessly to improve the infrastructure and quality of life in New York City. He bemoaned what he saw as the degeneration of the merchant class in the city and felt that qualities such as honor and honesty were becoming less prevalent as the century progressed. George believed that merchants had an obligation to rule the city and that aldermen should all be businessmen, too. He gave freely of his money, time and energy to ensure that politicians would be of his class and consciousness. Sometimes his money was not wisely spent, as in the time he invested thousands in Daniel Webster's presidential campaign. Although the Griswold brothers died shortly after mid-century, their progeny kept the family business intact until 1879.

Chapter 11

THE BLACK X LINE

The early nineteenth century saw a shift from government to commerce on the part of the Griswold family. John Griswold founded the Black X Line in 1823. It was among the first shipping lines to initiate packet service between New York and London. Named because it carried mail packets and adhered to a regular schedule, packet service revolutionized transatlantic travel and trade. Packet ships, their cargo and their passengers had a significant impact on the economic and social development of the eastern seaboard in the nineteenth century. The red, swallow-tailed pennant marked with an "X" flew proudly from the masts and was sewn onto the fore topsail of several important ships in the 1820s and '30s. Among them were the *Sovereign*, the *Cambria*, the *Hudson* and the *President*. The *President* was the first command of the legendary captain E.E. Morgan, who later became the manager and then owner of the Black X Line.

In an age when amiability was not usually a trait for which oceangoing captains were noted, Morgan was often depicted as a model of geniality. His easygoing demeanor was said to quell the consternation of many immigrants who had never made a sea passage before. He was an ardent participant in the game of draughts, a popular shipboard activity at the time. His casual equanimity could be disrupted by a disputed call in a spirited game. He was eminently quotable. One of his most famous *bon mots* occurred when Queen Victoria deigned to have lunch aboard her namesake Black X packet, the *Victoria*. When asked by the Duke of Newcastle why it took so long for the

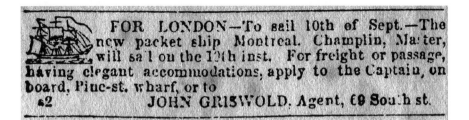

FOR LONDON—To sail 10th of Sept.—The new packet ship Montreal. Champlin, Master, will sail on the 10th inst. For freight or passage, having elegant accommodations, apply to the Captain, on board, Pine-st. wharf, or to
s2   JOHN GRISWOLD. Agent, 69 South st.

Advertisement for a Black X Line ship bound for England. *Griswold family archives.*

Americans to name a ship for the queen, Morgan replied, "We had to wait until there was one worthy of her."

The *Victoria* caused quite a stir at its launch. It was the first packet to incorporate several innovations that made the life of immigrants more comfortable. Built in 1844, it was the first of its kind to have a long poop that stretched farther than the mainmast. Beside it was a "house on deck" that allowed second-class passengers to travel in an airy, well-ventilated space, as opposed to the squalid, often-fetid conditions that existed below decks at the time. Such innovations made Black X vessels popular with European immigrants who were being pushed out of their old countries by political, religious, social and economic conditions. Thousands of people were transported to the streets-paved-with-gold shores of America.

Sending ships back and forth across the North Atlantic in the winter was an ongoing challenge to Griswold and his captains and crews. A typical winter voyage in a Black X packet was recorded in the journal of a passenger named Leslie, who wrote that the *Hudson* left New York in November 1842 very deeply laden with a mixed cargo. The ship drew eighteen feet fully loaded and had only five feet of freeboard. It was so full that Griswold gave his skipper a final word of warning to be very careful as he made his way across the ocean. A series of gales beset the ship as soon as it left port; it was pushed along by following seas. It made eight hundred miles in four days, which was very good time for a packet ship with low masts and rigging.

On the fourth day out, a huge sea overtook the ship, smashing the stern deadlights and sending six inches of water into the poop cabin. The helmsmen were washed from their posts, and the captain and the mate were able to grab the spinning wheel at the last moment to prevent a possibly fatal broaching to. After this close encounter, the captain wisely decided to heave to and ride out the gale in relative safety and comfort. Gale after gale continued to buffet the *Hudson* along, to the point that when it reached waters shallow enough to require soundings, only fifteen crewmen out of a compliment of twenty-five were in any condition to go aloft. The rigging had to be continually reinforced to prevent dismasting. During all this tumult, some casks of turpentine in the cargo hold were smashed, and their contents kept clogging up the pumps, adding to the already dangerous conditions.

The ten cabin passengers were forced to stay below decks for the entire passage. They spent their time playing an early version of modern-day blackjack called *vingt-et-un*. Their days and nights were filled with endless shouts of "I stand!" "Double all around!" and "Pay up!" interspersed with violent bouts of seasickness. The diary keeper bemoaned the boredom and monotony, interspersed with moments of terror and uncertainty, typical of an ocean passage under sail.

One moonless night, the gambler's card shufflings were interrupted with loud, panicked shouts of "Port! Port! Hard a port." The *Hudson* had run down and narrowly missed colliding with a bark that was lying to, waiting for better weather before continuing its voyage. In those days, ships carried no lights, and there are many stories of fishing boats on the Grand Banks being run down and sunk by packet ships as they hurried along across the Atlantic.

Ironically, after days of roaring gales that ultimately washed one crewman overboard and smashed in much of the upper bulwarks, the ship ran out of wind within sight of England and was forced to spend several days bobbing about within sight of land. It did not reach its berth until two days after Christmas. The return voyage to America was even worse. Facing wind and seas on its nose, the packet took seventy days to reach the East Coast from England. The *Hudson* served Griswold very well for thirteen more years until it foundered and broke up in the mid-Atlantic. Fortunately, another vessel came to its rescue, and all hands were saved to sail another day.

The Black X Line's most famous captain was a scion of Griswold Point. Robert Harper Griswold was the ninth of Governor Roger Griswold's ten children. Born in 1801, his nautical career was noted by several important people in the nineteenth century, including no less a commentator on the nautical scene than Herman Melville. Since his father was away from home so much, his mother was in charge of his early development. Robert was educated at the Black Hall School, where he later returned as a teacher.

Robert was destined for a maritime career; it seemed part of his birthright. He was shipping out as a mate while still in his teens, and by the time he was in his twenties, he was a packet ship captain. His first command was the *Samuel Robertson* on a voyage from Liverpool to New York. He spent the next twenty-five years on the quarterdeck of Atlantic packets. He was master of several

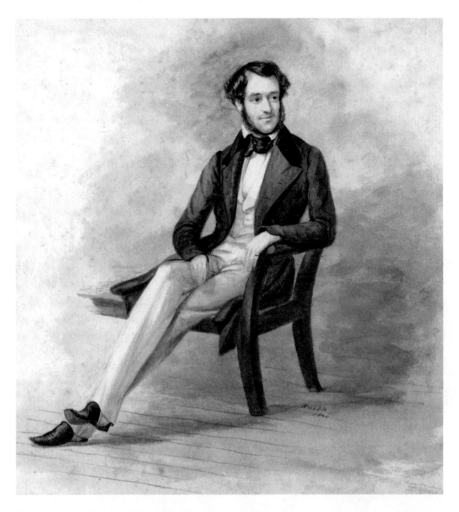

The legendary Captain Robert Harper Griswold. After a long career as a master mariner, he briefly taught at the Black Hall School. *Courtesy of the Florence Griswold Museum.*

Black X Liners, including the *Sovereign*, the *Toronto*, the *Northumberland*, the *Southampton* and the *Ocean Queen*. His career spanned the final years in which sail was the primary means of propulsion for ships crossing the Atlantic.

It was as a cabin passenger aboard the *Southampton* that the premier maritime author of the nineteenth century, Herman Melville, kept a journal of his trip from New York to London. Melville's insights provide a vivid portrait of Griswold's seamanship and character. Griswold was ideally suited to be a genial host to his passengers. A family book states that he "was a man of much reading, and in his prime, of elegant manners and great personal beauty." He presided over a table that featured good food and plenty of it, excellent wines and lively discussions on a wide range of topics. The cabin passengers, like Melville, enjoyed a quality of shipboard life that was in marked contrast to the cramped conditions and monotonous food of the third-class passengers below decks. After a rough start to the voyage that inspired much seasickness, the weather improved, and the ship made good time across the Atlantic.

Melville was a favorite of the captain, and Griswold honored him with a stateroom all his own, a boon in those days when most had to share living space, often with strangers. Melville was effusive in his praise of his quarters. He found them to be almost as large as his room at home. The sofa, washstand and large berth were much to his liking. The large mirror in his cabin allowed him to keep track of his splendid beard, of which he was quite proud. Melville felt quite special to be singled out by Captain Griswold and blessed with a cabin all to himself.

Life aboard a Black X packet wasn't quite as pleasant for the passengers in third-class below decks, who were crammed into tight quarters with poor ventilation, segregated by gender and given monotonous food. Melville relates that one of them jumped overboard and drowned. The man's wife said that there was no use trying to save him, as there were plenty of other available men on board! Captain Griswold noted that the man was one of four or five passengers who leaped to a watery end during his time at sea.

Melville said that the captain's mood always improved when the wind was fair, which seems to be a reasonable assumption. He relates various pranks and hijinks pulled by the passengers to keep the captain on his toes and the passengers entertained. One such was a debate that tried to resolve which was better, a democracy or a monarchy. To his chagrin, the British cabin passengers refused to participate. As a result, the debate was not as fiery and contentious as Melville and his fellow Americans might have hoped. But the incident underscores the tricky social waters that a packet captain had to navigate with passengers from both sides of the Atlantic who came from countries still not quite at peace with one another.

Captain Griswold was highly regarded by Melville, who called him a very intelligent and gentlemanly fellow. He considered Griswold to be an excellent conversationalist who was well aware of his positions on issues and could ably defend them. After they arrived safely in England, the captain, Melville and some other passengers would dine together and tip back a few ardent spirits. Melville recalled a pub crawl to the Judge and

Jury on Bow Street, which he sums up as "exceedingly diverting, but not superlatively moral." It is, perhaps, one of the best summaries of a pub crawl written in the English language. Melville gave Captain Griswold a book in appreciation for his attentions and courtesies, and the captain wrote him a bread-and-butter note in return.

Helen, Robert's wife, would occasionally cross the Atlantic with her husband, bringing along their children when possible. But the nature of Robert's business caused him to necessarily be away from home and miss some holidays and important family events. One of those events occurred on a holiday when their daughter, Florence, was born on Christmas morning in 1850. Florence went on to become an important part of America's culture, history and heritage. But like thousands of other sailors' wives, Helen would miss her husband terribly when he was away at sea. In several letters, she laments the lack of his presence and the travails of raising a family without him.

After the *Southampton*, Griswold took command of the *Ocean Queen*. During his tenure aboard this ship, the number of immigrants crossing the Atlantic to America grew considerably. Economic and political upheavals in Europe, coupled with the promise of economic and social upward mobility in America, pushed and pulled people to fill the tenements and factories of the eastern seaboard. These people, who braved an Atlantic crossing, provided the human power necessary to build and sustain the Industrial Revolution.

The Black X Ship *American Eagle* in heavy seas. *Griswold family archives.*

Visitors to the Florence Griswold Museum are greeted by the sight of this beautifully restored house. *Author's collection.*

The immigrants also headed west to push the borders of manifest destiny and build the heartland's agricultural empire. At one point, the *Ocean Queen* was carrying upward of six hundred immigrants per each westbound passage. It was ultimately lost with all hands, including its new captain, W.B. Smith, in a winter gale off the Isle of Wight in 1856.

Griswold retired from the sea at the age of forty-nine, as the Age of Sail was evolving into the Age of Steam. He proudly purchased the Noyes House on Lyme Street, the finest residence in the town. Once ashore, he invested in several Old Lyme businesses, including a nail manufactory, a blacksmith shop and a dam with a waterworks. He accumulated a modest fortune and went on to become a leading member of Lyme society. Unfortunately, his economic circumstances, along with those of Old Lyme, diminished significantly as the result of the Civil War. At the time of his death, his once healthy estate was reduced significantly.

Chapter 12

CAPTAIN JOHN GRISWOLD

The Civil War was more heartily supported by New Englanders than was the War of 1812. In keeping with the family's military tradition, John Griswold, the youngest son of Colonel Charles Chandler and Ellen Griswold, volunteered to serve in support of the Union cause. John has been described as a "Renaissance man" by John Banks in his excellent book *Connecticut Yankees at Antietam* (The History Press). He was fluent in several languages and was a consummate athlete, noted for his fencing skills. He was as serious student of both the arts and the sciences. Banks's comprehensive narrative traces John's early years from his graduation from Yale in 1857, his work as a surveyor in the Midwest and his travels to the islands of the Pacific.

Griswold was in Hawaii on business when armed hostilities between the North and the South broke out. He took a ship across the Pacific and then traveled on stagecoaches and trains until he arrived back in Old Lyme in 1861. His intention was to enlist immediately as a private in the Union army, but his family and friends convinced him that his knowledge and skills would be more useful to the Northern cause if he were to become an officer instead. Governor William Buckingham agreed that he should become a commissioned officer and suggested that he form a company of men from the shoreline region of the state. On New Year's Eve 1861, John Griswold became a captain in Company 1 of the Eleventh Connecticut Volunteers. The die that would propel him toward his heroic end had been cast.

A fervent patriot, Griswold came to meet that end on September 17, 1862, the "bloodiest day in U.S. history." It was on that day that the Battle of Antietam took place on the bank of Antietam Creek. Around ten o'clock that morning, 440 Connecticut soldiers, under the command of Colonel Henry Kingsbury, charged down the slope toward what became known as Burnside's Bridge in hopes of routing its Georgia defenders. Such a rout was not to be, however. Despite strong artillery support directed by Kingsbury's West Point classmate Lieutenant Samuel Benjamin, the Eleventh Connecticut was exposed to the withering fire of Georgia sharpshooters. Well positioned behind stone walls and in trees and well equipped with smoothbores and Enfield rifles, the Rebels poured volley after volley of .577- and .69-caliber bullets into the vulnerable blue line.

From his position behind a stone wall that afforded scant protection, Captain Griswold realized the dire circumstances that his troops found themselves in and decided that drastic action had to be taken to avert a massacre. He formed a plan to lead his men directly across Antietam Creek rather than surge toward the narrow bridge that could well have been a fatal trap. He stood up in plain view of the Confederate snipers and encouraged his troops to follow him toward a shallow spot that he thought could be easily crossed. Waving his saber and shouting, Griswold vaulted the stone wall and rallied his men to follow him into the creek.

Although the water wasn't very deep, the Connecticut Yankees had a difficult time finding their footing in the stream due to underwater tree limbs, rocks and mud. The gray-clad Confederates took full advantage of their enemy's diminished mobility and opened up with a firestorm of bullets. As they neared the far bank, the current began to course more swiftly, and the mud became deeper and muckier, further impeding their progress. They became even easier targets for the Georgia boys—almost literally sitting ducks.

Slogging through thick mud, fighting a strong current and heading directly toward the entrenched enemy, Captain Griswold and his men took a horrendous number of casualties. At midstream, waving his saber to exhort his troops forward, Captain Griswold was struck by multiple bullets. In spite of his grievous wounds, the Union officer managed to make it to the western shore of the river. Confederate lore holds that sharpshooters were so impressed with his heroic efforts that they held their fire when Griswold reached land. By then, of course, virtually every bluecoat who had followed him into the water had been killed or wounded.

As Griswold lay dying on the riverbank, some enlisted men under his command ran to summon his friend Nathan Mayer, who was one of the regiment's medical doctors. The medic forded the creek to reach his fallen

Captain John Griswold's bravery at Antietam was noted by both Union and Confederate soldiers. *Author's collection.*

friend and helped his men carry him to a nearby outbuilding. Dr. Mayer treated the injured Connecticut captain with morphine but quickly realized that Griswold's wounds were fatal. Ever the gentleman, the captain thanked Dr. Mayer for his friendship and medical attention, but he felt that the doctor's attention should be focused on the other wounded men who were filing into the building.

Major General Ambrose Burnside, Griswold's commanding officer, who was having an exceedingly busy day, rushed to be at the young officer's side. Burnside and Griswold were purported to be friends. The captain told the general that it was an honor to die for his country and that he was a happy man, despite his painful circumstances. General Burnside wept openly when he learned of his comrade's death the following day.

Griswold's bravery and bonhomie were eulogized and long remembered. Family and friends recalled him not only as a brave hero in combat but also as a sensitive, thoughtful man. He was a scientist who could quote classical literature. He was deeply respected by the men who served under him. They remembered him as an officer who treated them with equanimity and good humor. Family members recalled him as a loving son and a good younger brother. He was laid to rest in the family cemetery on the bank of the Black Hall River. It is a poetic resting place, considering his trials and tribulations trying to reach the banks of Antietam Creek. His grave is marked with a monument hewn from Portland Brownstone. The monument was widely held to be an outstanding example of the stonecutter's craft and was highly praised as such at the time of its creation. Even today, John Griswold's memory lies deep in the emotions of family members. When relating his ancestor's heroics, Matthew Griswold X misted up when he repeated the brave captain's last words: "Tell my mother I died at the head of my company."

Chapter 13

FLORENCE GRISWOLD

A fter the Civil War, sea captain Robert Harper Griswold, of the Black X Line, left his widow and four children the grand house on Lyme Street and several acres of adjacent land on the banks of the Lieutenant River. His widow, Helen, was left with three daughters and a son. Sadly, the son, Robert Jr., died of diphtheria at a young age. Rocked by this tragedy and economic uncertainties, the remaining Griswold women opened the Griswold Home School in 1878, when daughter Florence was twenty-eight. They offered instruction in foreign language, music and the arts. The school helped the family survive, but it wasn't enough to keep the four women totally afloat financially. In order to supplement their income, they also opened their home to boarders. This turned out to be a most propitious decision for Miss Florence, the town of Old Lyme and the world of art and culture.

As the nineteenth century waned, Florence's older sister, who was the organist for the Congregational Church, and their mother passed on to their Christian rewards. Florence and her sister Adele struggled on, trying to maintain themselves by running their boardinghouse and sometimes selling the plants, flowers and vegetables that bloomed in their garden. In 1899, a boarder came to the house who changed the scope and character of Miss Florence's world. His name was Henry Ward Ranger, and he was an artist. Ward was quite taken with his quarters and with the very paintable scenes that Old Lyme and its natural environs offered to his discerning eye and palette. He put the word out to his fellow painters, and they began to flock to the Griswold House. As a result, one of the most productive art colonies in America began to flourish. There, American impressionists found a convivial and inspirational atmosphere in which to create some of the most beautiful art of the early twentieth century. Such notables of the brush as Childe Hassam, Frank Dumond and William Metcalf called Miss Florence's house their home away from home.

Many other significant painters stayed at her fecund art colony throughout the years, including Wilson Irvine and Edward Charles Voelkert. Voelkert, along with William Henry Howe, was famous for his paintings of cattle, and the farms around Old Lyme provided him with many examples of New England bovinity. Matilda Browne and the sisters Breta and Lydia Longacre were prominent female artists who stayed with Miss Florence. Ellen Axson Wilson, the first wife of President Woodrow Wilson, was also an occasional resident, and she became a close friend and confidant of its proprietor, known to all as Miss Florence.

Florence enjoyed a long, active and productive life. She was at the center of a wide circle of very talented and creative friends. She was quite active in local affairs and worked tirelessly on behalf of the town she loved. Heeding the advice of President Wilson's wife and other friends, she created a gallery in the front of her house to exhibit and sell paintings and antiques. Some of her civic activities included spearheading a grassroots group to prevent a trolley line from running down Lyme Street. She was also a founding member of the Old Lyme Fire Department. When the Lyme Art Association opened a gallery next to her house on property she donated, it selected her to be its manager. She received a commission on the art sold by the association.

Alas, all these endeavors were not enough to sustain Miss Florence economically. Deeply in debt, her many artist friends, under the leadership of her cousin and personal physician Dr. Matthew Griswold (Matthew IX), banded together to form the Florence Griswold Association with the intention of buying her property, settling her outstanding bills and providing an income to support her for the rest of her life. They were outbid by a lawyer from New York with Old Lyme roots, who purchased her house and land. He built a house for himself and his family on the property. He generously stipulated that Florence would be welcome to live in her family home for the rest of her life.

Florence died in 1937, when the country was mired deeply in the Great Depression, but lives on in one of the country's and, for that matter, one of the world's most elegant and aesthetic museums of art. Today, the Florence Griswold Museum is a premier destination for artists and art lovers from around the globe. Its collections rank among the very best, especially among those that focus on American impressionism. It houses fine art, sculpture, ephemera, studio material, toys and dolls, furniture, textiles, decorative arts and historical materials. Located on its beautiful grounds on the banks of the Lieutenant River, it is a centerpiece of the Old Lyme community, providing not only economic benefit from the many tourists and art lovers who visit every year but also a vibrant matrix that nourishes and inspires the spirit of the town and its visitors and residents.

Chapter 14

THE BLACK HALL SCHOOL

At the beginning of the nineteenth century, several prominent residents of Black Hall came together to create a school that would be dedicated to providing the area's children with an educational experience that would facilitate their matriculation into college and instill in them the social graces. The initial subscribers who created the school included Governor Roger Griswold, Judge Matthew Griswold, Deacon John Griswold, Diodate Griswold and Lee Lay. This committee set in motion the administrative wherewithal to create a little wooden schoolhouse that was exceedingly tiny by today's standards. During its more than one hundred years of operation, the Black Hall School would educate not only the children of Old Lyme but also boarders from all over the East Coast.

The original document that created the school reads:

> *We the subscribers agree to build a schoolhouse for the eighth district in the first society of Lyme, of the following subscription...is to be seventeen feet in length and fourteen feet in width in the clear, and to be seven and one half feet between the joints, to be covered with pine board as high as the desks and plastered with lime mortar above the overhead. It is to have three windows and an outside door to open into and entry by the side of the chimney.*

The schoolhouse had magnificent views of Long Island Sound and the Back, Black Hall and Connecticut Rivers. It overlooked a section of the water known as Devil's Bend, said to be equal to the English Channel in

The original Black Hall School. *Griswold family archives.*

terms of the amount of commercial boat traffic that passed through it. Students catching a glimpse out the window in an idle moment could also gaze upon fertile fields and look across the river to the village of Saybrook. Ships of the West Indies trade could be seen heading upriver with cargoes of rum and molasses, or downriver filled with salted shad, onions and lumber.

The connection between the Black Hall School and seafaring was reinforced by the presence of former shipmasters as members of its faculty. Exalted captains Augustus Henry Griswold and William Griswold both served as teachers at the Black Hall School. Augustus Henry was asked to bring some semblance of discipline to the student body during the winter of 1830. It seems that the young scholars at the time had driven their teacher out of the school—and probably out of the teaching profession altogether. The captain stepped into the breach for the princely sum of eight dollars a month. When he made his first appearance in the classroom, he quickly made it known in no uncertain terms that he was in command of that deck. Years later, student reminiscences recalled his no-nonsense approach to education and "the light that shone from Captain Griswold's eyes."

Captain William Griswold also served as a teacher at Black Hall School. He had made several voyages on the quarterdeck of N.L. and G. Griswold China clippers and was also a stickler for student discipline. There was a requirement that a search committee vet prospective candidates for teaching positions. Legend has it that when the captain, with his significant Asian adventures behind him, appeared before the committee, he was asked only one question:

Captain Augustus Henry Griswold commanded Black X Line packet ships across the Atlantic. *Courtesy of Murray Wilmerding.*

"Where is Canton?" The stalwart seafarer passed that quiz with all flags flying, and he assumed command of his classroom the following day.

In commemoration of the school's centennial in 1906, Matthew Griswold VII was asked to share some of what he remembered from his Black Hall School days. He recalled that he was an early admission because four years of age was the minimum for attendance, and he was "just half past three." This was in 1836, and the school was packed full of students. To accommodate so young and small a child, Griswold's father fashioned a small seat, which was "placed under the desk next to the door, where the bench used by the older students was cut short." He remembers his teacher as a "quaint and singular character, quite a collector of odds and ends." The much put upon educator began every conversation and every entry in his journal with the words "I awoke this morning with a slight headache."

Griswold also spoke highly of two of the school's female teachers—Miss Sargent, whom he praised as being "one of the best teachers ever employed there," and Miss Swan, whom he called a "fine teacher beloved of the pupils." He was considerably less fond of a teacher named Henry Haynes, who he noted was "a well-known player of the clarinet. As a child, I said if I ever grew up, I would surely kill him, but I grew up and did not kill him; instead we became good friends and I enjoyed his music. The cause of my anger was the continued, almost daily punishment he seemed to take delight in giving me. I was seven, and felt it was undeserved."

Matthew didn't get any special treatment in the discipline department from his uncle Captain William Griswold. Matthew noted, "His method of classroom governance was partly moral suasion, quite largely of the quince sprouts. [Quince sprouts apparently make good switches for caning students.] Students were forced to harvest their own instruments of punishment. The 'Lower Garden' furnished a convenient and abundant supply of very long and fine 'tinglers.' I have taken many of these as I went along to school, at Uncle's command, feeling some of them afterwards."

At the other end of the disciplinary spectrum was a "wonderful teacher" who let his young scholars "do as we pleased…and we were pleased to do many queer things. A favorite pastime during school hours was to hang ourselves out of the windows, with feet swinging, like so many imps hung out to dry." The harried teacher sent notes home to parents in hope of enlisting their aid in quelling the student "insurrections." The student insurgents countered this move by burying the notes instead of delivering them. The teacher's tenure was short-lived; however, he went on to create a patent medicine called "Champion's Lina-Mentum, which had quite a large sale and was a really good remedy for cuts and bruises."

Griswold waxes poetic in his summation of the benefits of Black Hall School, writing, "No doubt the time spent in this old school house had its influence for good, and did its share in forming character that helped [its students] stand for the right. Who dares dispute the statement that the school houses of New England have been the means of forming the character and giving force to the magnificent race of people which made

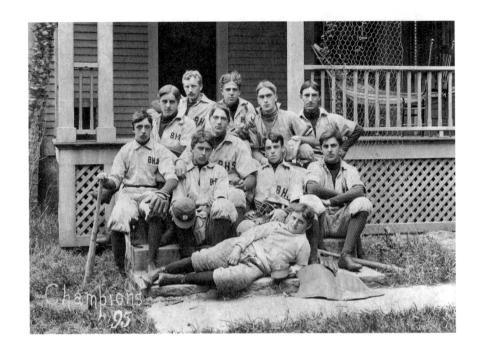

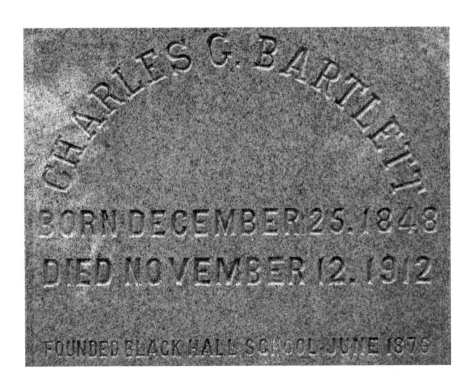

New England the head and front of the great country we now call ours? Words fail, when the attempt is made, to over shadow the mighty force and power of the school house."

In 1876, Charles Griswold Bartlett transformed this basic schoolhouse into a private educational facility for boys aged ten years and older. According to Bartlett, "The object of the school is to afford to a limited number of boys thorough preparations for any college or scientific school… and to promote their physical development by means of systematic training and out-door sports of all kinds, and to make them manly, Christian men." Bartlett touted the school's easy railroad access to New York. At the beginning of the twentieth century, he boasted that "a local and long distance telephone connects the school with all points reached by wire; and telegrams are transmitted by telephone to and from the telegraph office at Lyme Ferry."

A flurry of construction replaced the one-room school. As Bartlett noted, "The school rooms are large, light and well ventilated. The sleeping rooms are arranged so that two boys room together, each of whom has a bed, washstand, bureau and closet of his own. There are bath rooms with hot and cold water in each wing." A Boynton hot-water system kept the scholars warm. Each boy had his very own radiator, ensuring a "mild, even temperature." The sanitation system received the blessing of the Secretary of the State Board of Health. The gym also featured a Boynton heating system, and the dressing room was adjacent to it. Bartlett added, "[With] everything under the same roof, there is no danger from exposure to cold or dampness when [the boys are] heated from exercise."

Bartlett was proud of BHS's healthy environment. In his words, "The health of the school has always been excellent. But, should illness break out, a boy can be kept with his nurse in quiet and entirely isolated from the other members of the school. A matron is also at hand, whose prompt and judicious treatment seldom fails to cure minor ailments." BHS was portrayed as place where a boy's mind, body and character could develop in a healthy atmosphere.

Opposite, top: The Black Hall School baseball team, 1895. W.E.S. Griswold is at the center of the picture. *Griswold family archives.*

Opposite, bottom: Charles Griswold Bartlett founded the Black Hall School. *Author's collection.*

The Black Hall School encouraged physical fitness as well as intellectual and moral prowess. *Griswold family archives.*

Academically, the school's aim was to prepare boys for college by means of a "system of individual instruction combined with recitations in small classes, so that each boy has the special care and drill that he needs." Class participation was valued and rewarded. While there was a structured curriculum, there was also accommodation for those who didn't quite fit the mold: "Those who cannot be rigidly classified without detriment to their progress may study such branches as their parents select…but each boy must take such an amount of work as will…give him sufficient employment during school hours."

Parents were urged to follow the academic calendar due to the "long vacations and short terms that have become the custom in our modern system of education." Students were required to learn how to sight-read Greek and Latin beginning at an early age. They were also expected to have some command of French and German. Those lax in their language recitations had to make them up during recreation hours. The practice of sending home report cards was discontinued because it was seen as old-fashioned: "Such reports, as all who give thought to the matter know, are at best but half-truths." Instead, the principal would send parents special reports from time to time, should they be warranted.

The Black Hall River Bridge in its current manifestation. Oil on canvas by Frederick Schavoir. *Photo by author.*

The school's certificate was accepted by Cornell, Brown, Amherst and Williams in lieu of examinations. It had a special arrangement with Yale, which invited parents of prospective students to get in touch with the faculty for further clarification. It is clear, however, that completion of the Black Hall program pretty much guaranteed acceptance into a top-tier college.

The students' day began with a bell at 7:00 a.m., followed by prayer, breakfast, classes until 1:00 p.m., dinner, sports, study hall, supper, more classes and lights out at 10:00 p.m. Sundays were devoted to the spiritual development of the boys, who were required to attend a church service in the morning, study the Bible in the afternoon and participate in a responsive service of prayer and praise in the evening.

Physical training was mandatory unless excused due to special circumstances. Daily exercise took place during the winter months. In keeping with the seasons, baseball, football and track were the primary sports. Access to the nearby estuary of the Connecticut River allowed students to row and sail "under the best and safest conditions." A skating pond was flooded to a depth of two feet or less for safety's sake. Gymnastics and tennis were also available to the boys. Bartlett stresses that "great care is taken that athletic interests may not encroach upon studies, and many of the best athletes of the school have been among its best scholars."

A strong body is best if it houses a sharp mind and character of good moral fiber. BHS aimed to combine good scholarship with the refinements of a

> *pleasant, healthy, Christian home. The discipline and moral training of the boys…are the special care of the principal. The members of the school are sons of gentlemen and are expected to conduct themselves as such. While rules are necessary and strictly enforced, the boys are put on their honor, and everything is done to foster truth and manly candor. Especially their moral natures are not cramped by any system of espionage. Any boy who is unfit to mingle with the upright, or has a problem with discipline, will be removed from the body.*

This excellent education came with a price tag, however. Tuition and board cost $500.00 per year. There was also a charge of $0.75 for every item of clothing washed, and a seat in church went for $4.00. For an extra $200.00 per year, a boy could get a single room and avoid the stresses that came with having a roommate. Damage to private rooms was the responsibility of the occupant, but common room damage was paid for by the school unless the perps were identified. If they could pay the freight, boys were also expected to bring their own "napkin ring, slippers, overshoes, rubber boots, rubber coat, blankets and towels."

Chapter 15

POTS AND PANS

As of this writing, the most collectible cast-iron products in the world have the name "GRISWOLD" proudly stamped onto them. There are societies of collectors that specialize in Griswold products. EBay trades them daily. Entire books are dedicated to collecting and preserving them. Conventions and shows are held around the country featuring the products of the family foundry. Countless millions of eggs have been fried in Griswold skillets. They still are quite serviceable a century and a half after they were first manufactured. Just as Griswolds played an integral role in nineteenth-century oceanic transportation, the frying pan was the family's contribution to the manufacturing megalith that allowed the United States to play the premier role in the Industrial Revolution.

Matthew VII was born at Black Hall on June 6, 1833, the son of Matthew VI and Phoebe Ely Griswold. He was the only male out of eight children. His father, Matthew VI, had begun the study of medicine, but the sudden death of his father compelled him to return to the family estate at Black Hall to farm and take care of his mother and his growing brood. Matthew VII spent the first thirty years of his life in Old Lyme. In keeping with the family tradition of public service, he served in the Connecticut state legislature. He married Sarah Olmstead, a member of one of the founding families of Erie, Pennsylvania. His grandson George Turnure Griswold, writing in *J.S. Griswold: Ancestors and Descendants* in 1995, had the following to say about this captain of Erie industry:

Matthew Griswold
VII. *Photo by Ray Guasp.*

A word should be said about the character and abilities of Matthew Griswold, founder of the Erie Griswold clan. Above all, he was a strongly humanistic family man who enjoyed life to the utmost. He was temperate and was known not only for his great sense of humor, but also for his entrepreneurial ability. The latter took him not only into a vastly successful foundry business, but also into banking and the manufacture of pianos. Throughout his life he had an enduring interest in politics and was elected to two terms in Congress. Within the family it has often been said that he would have been a much better businessman had he not been so kind hearted, a philosophy modern-day entrepreneurs might well contemplate should they be so inclined.

The story of his remarkable Matthew VII's cast-iron company began in 1865, when he followed his wife to Pennsylvania and entered into partnership with J.C. and Samuel Selden to form the Selden and Griswold Manufacturing Company. Their operation was known as the "Butt Factory" because they began making butt hinges and other light hardware. Their factory was located on Tenth and Chestnut Streets on the banks of the Erie Extension Canal. Later, they moved to the corners of Twelfth and Raspberry Streets. Griswold bought out the Selden interest in 1884, and the company was renamed the Griswold Manufacturing Company. Around this time, the company began to make aluminum cookware, beginning with teapots. It kept the Griswold name long past the time of Matthew's death in 1919. After being widowed by Sarah Olmstead, Matthew had married Annie Schenk. Two of their sons, Roger and Ely Griswold, went on to serve as presidents of the Griswold Manufacturing Company. Anna Schenk Griswold took a notable camping trip throughout the West in 1871. Her journals of this trip were published in *Colorado Magazine* in the summer of 1965.

The Griswold foundry made many innovative products to fill the everyday needs of America's burgeoning population. It tried to create and fill niches in the homes and businesses necessitated by the seemingly never-ending influx of immigrants. Among the more creative of these endeavors was its design and patent of a cuspidor on casters that could easily be moved about to accommodate the often-unreliable aims of the tobacco-chewing public. It also manufactured such varied items as stovepipe dampers, trivets, thimbles, waffle irons, pots, kettles, grinding mills and tobacco cutters. Such kitchen staples as kettles, Dutch ovens, gridirons and roasters also rolled out of the Griswold factory.

Always amenable to innovation and new challenges, Matthew Griswold was approached in 1889 by a young engineer who had formulated a process to make the casting of aluminum affordable and efficient. Legend has it that Matthew was intrigued by the idea but not quite sure about what to make as a prototype. He received his answer when he asked his secretary what light and handy kitchen implement a woman would most want. Her reply was, "A teapot!" The Griswold line of aluminum cookware was the result.

As the young country's transportation networks grew and improved, Griswold salesmen, in the tradition of Yankee peddlers, took their products to the far reaches of the North, South and West. Their scope ultimately extended from Maine to California, Michigan to Florida and beyond. Ambitious distributors, who bought trainloads of products at a time, even shipped them to Europe and Asia on the steamships that had replaced the

Anna Schenk Griswold takes her first plane ride. *Griswold family archives.*

Anna Scheck Griswold and husband, Matthew, relaxing in their later years. *Griswold family archives.*

packets and clippers of the Age of Sail. In the 1880s, the company expanded its line to include large commercial products for restaurants and commercial kitchens. Well into the twentieth century, it marketed complete kitchenware packages designed to cook for one family or hundreds of people.

Perhaps the most famous of Griswold's employees was a redoubtable woman fondly referred to by her public as Aunt Ellen. Her real name was Etta Moses, and she was an expert on cooking with Griswold cookware. She would share recipes and techniques with her adoring fan base, even creating a cookbook written specifically for the company's products. Her cookbook was popular for decades and went through several reprints. She would include pamphlets with new products that would have handy hints, such as how to cure and dry a skillet properly, as well as recipes and other cooking ideas. Aunt Etta received stacks of mail every day and tried as best she could to answer as many of them as possible.

The company began to enamel its cookware in the 1920s and also began electrifying some of its products. The company was sold to a syndicate of New York investors in 1947; by that time, no family members were associated with the operation. The company was beset by labor and economic problems, including increased competition from other manufacturers. It went through several corporate changes before closing operations in Erie in 1957. In 1969, General Housewares Corp. acquired all rights to the Griswold name.

Matthew did not limit his manufacturing genius to metal implements. In 1890, he organized the Shaw Piano Company. An advertising card for the company boasted, "No piano has achieved the popularity in so short time as the Matchless Shaw Piano. Why? Because it is built upon honor, sold upon merit, and possesses that sympathetic quality of tone, combined with power and lasting musical qualities found in no other piano. Musical in every fiber. The acknowledged peer among pianos. See these beauties." Unfortunately, the company's finances did not strike a pleasant chord with its creditors, and Shaw Piano was forced into bankruptcy ten years after its founding.

Not only was Matthew an industrialist after his move to Pennsylvania, but he also pursued his interest in public service. He was a longtime trustee of the Erie Academy. He also revived the family presence on the floor of the U.S. House of Representatives and was elected to the Fifty-second and Fifty-fourth Congresses on the Republican ticket. Fortunately, he was able to keep a lid on Griswold pugnacity and did not engage in any fisticuffs while in the halls of Congress.

His son, Matthew VIII, also served as president of the Griswold cast-iron company. He also played a key role in bringing the General Electric

Company to Erie. A Yale classmate of his named Pratt was the engineer for GE charged with selecting a site between Buffalo and Cleveland for the company's new plant. Griswold hosted him with good cheer and became a one-man lobbying committee for his hometown of Erie. He cited its great railroad access and water resources, noting that its location on the shores of Lake Erie made it accessible to several forms of water transportation and that the shale underlying the area would be a solid base for such a large facility. Griswold was ultimately successful in persuading Pratt to put his plant in Erie, and he eventually became the facility's manager. He also was instrumental in bringing the New York Central and Pennsylvania Railroads to the area, as well as a main branch of the U.S. Post Office. The post office site at Fourteenth and Peach Streets was named Griswold Place in his honor.

As a last hurrah, in 1951, the Griswold Manufacturing Company put together a float for Erie's Bicentennial Parade. Approximately three thousand paperweights in the shape of a dog were cast to be distributed to the crowd. Two thousand of them were given away that day, and the rest were presented to company employees, distributors and customers as a token of thanks for their hard work and patronage. Today, Griswold #30 pups are highly sought-after collectibles. All Griswold Manufacturing products are prized for their antique value and usefulness. They continue to increase in worth as time goes by. Among the reasons for this is the fact that they can be accurately dated by their markings and that they are still serviceable as well as aesthetically decorative.

Other branches of the Griswold family made contributions to nineteenth- and early twentieth-century manufacturing. Thomas Griswold of New Orleans made swords for Confederate army and navy officers, much to the consternation of the officers and crew of the *George Griswold* when it was captured off the coast of Brazil. Griswold's artistic designs resulted in some of the most desirable Civil War artifacts (both real and counterfeit) that are currently being bandied about on television's *Antiques Roadshow*.

Another Griswold played an important role in arming the Confederacy. Samuel Griswold, a Connecticut native, moved to Georgia and developed an industrial area known as Griswoldville. His primary products were cotton gins, but he also made candles, soap and tallow. When hostilities with the North broke out, Samuel offered Griswoldville as a mustering point for Rebel troops. He retooled his factory to produce pistols instead of cotton-processing machinery, an ironic reversal of beating plowshares into swords. Griswold's town was burned by Yankee infantry in 1864. The Battle of Griswoldville was the first conflagration set off on Sherman's March to the Sea.

Griswolds also played a role in the development of the automobile industry in America. In 1907, the Griswold Motor Car Company created a roadster with a "unique vertical motor crankshaft and a symmetrical friction drive." The cars were built in Quincy, Massachusetts, and Troy, New York. They were marketed in 1908 but received underwhelming response from the motoring public. The company was eventually sold to the Bloomstrom Company, which marketed the Griswold under the name Gyroscope. It went out of business shortly after the transfer.

Another Griswold was much more successful in the automotive field. In the 1890s, M.E. Griswold started manufacturing bicycles out of stamped sheet metal. This new manufacturing technique was ideal for bicycles, and Griswold's company built and sold them under the names Independence and Prairie King. However, Griswold had entered the bicycle business arena just as the cycling fad was beginning to fade. Realizing that the future was unfolding in the burgeoning automobile craze, he moved his operation to Detroit and began making car bodies and parts. His work was first class, and he soon became sought after by several automobile manufacturers. He produced bodies for Columbia Motors, Palmer, Partin-Palmer, Wyllis-Knight and King Automobiles. He also made and sold prefabricated truck bodies so that his customers could assemble them at their sites.

By the 1920s, Griswold was specializing in open-car bodies such as phaetons, roadsters and convertibles. His company developed specialized techniques that resulted in fewer leaks and less rattling and drafts. It also invented a new fabric for convertibles and a window channel that proved to be much more waterproof than previous technologies.

As the Depression loomed, Griswold pinned his hopes on a revolutionary design for the Auburn Company known as the Cabin Speedster. Based on the aerodynamic style of airplanes, the Speedster featured a lightweight aluminum body, wicker seats, a radically canted windshield, cycle fenders that turned the wheels and a ducktail deck. The prototype of the car was a sensation at the New York Automobile Show in 1929. In February of that year, it was shown at the Los Angeles Show. In a terrible twist of fate, faulty wiring set the auditorium on fire, and all the cars, including the Cabin Speedster, were destroyed. Griswold's last production runs were for Wyllis-Knight in 1929, when the company produced both phaeton and roadster models. But the looming Depression and the popularity of closed automobiles spelled the end for Griswold's company, which went out of business in 1930.

The Griswold name is carried on a wide variety of products available today. These include HVAC controls, sponge rubber and urethane foam, water systems, pumps and filters. The popularity of several comedy movies featuring Chevy Chase as a zany Griswold sparked an endeavor much larger than a cottage industry that can be found on the Internet hawking T-shirts, coffee mugs, baseball caps, posters, stickers, postcards, sweatshirts, tote bags, refrigerator magnets, beer mugs, greeting cards, bumper stickers, calendars and mouse pads. This downward spiral from cookware to flapdoodle could well be a metaphor for the decline of our culture and the inevitable descent from classy to schlock that pervades the fabric of our society today.

Chapter 16

A COUNTRY DOCTOR

The Griswolds migrated back from Erie, Pennsylvania, and became fixtures in the Old Lyme community. It was a bit of an adjustment for some of the younger family members, who were convinced that milk came directly from nice, clean bottles left on a doorstep rather than from "dirty old cows." One of those youngsters was Matthew IX, who came to be known as Dr. Matt, a well-loved physician on the shoreline back when doctors still made house calls and actually knew their patients' names. Following in the footsteps of many of his ancestors, he attended Yale University. Although he was scheduled to graduate in 1918, World War I interfered, and his class graduated early so that they could rush to the battlefields of Europe.

Before he made it to Europe, Dr. Matt had some adventures stateside. After his induction into the service, it was found that he had a condition known as hammertoe, which would have made him ineligible for combat duty. The military's clever solution to the problem was to cut off his toes and send him to Texas for cavalry training. There, while astride a horse, practicing charges with saber held high, a ricocheting bullet hit his horse, missing Matt by less than two inches and killing his noble steed.

Much to the chagrin of his mother, and other mothers of Yale men in his company, Matt was posted to Mexico to receive artillery training. The consternation on the part of the worried mothers was a commonly held belief that any healthy, young American male who stepped foot across the Mexican border would immediately be stricken with a "social disease," a euphemism for an STD back in the early twentieth century. Fortunately,

The Black Hall Reporter

Vol. IV. No. 4.   BLACK HALL, SEPT. 24, 1927   Ten cents

COMPLIMENTS OF

The Griswold Manufacturing Co.

Griswold Extra Finished
Iron and Aluminum Cooking Utensils

Richard Ely

Golf Lessons for Beginners

THE BLACK HALL PRINTING CO.

Light Job Printing and
Publisher of The Black Hall Reporter

Above: Dr. Matt's House. Oil on canvas by Frederick Schavoir. *Photo by author.*

Opposite: The *Black Hall Reporter* was published from the 1920s through the 1950s. This 1927 issue complains about "alarming noise from automobiles." *Griswold family archives.*

most of the troopers managed to avoid that peril and were shipped across the Atlantic to France.

Because of his artillery training, Matt was assigned as an observer in a barrage balloon, reporting on enemy positions and directing Allied fire. They would have to ascend before dawn so as not to give away their launch position, and they couldn't descend until after dark. That made for a cold day, high up over France stuck in the confines of a small, wicker basket. This afforded the men little protection should they be attacked by airplanes, but airplanes were in short supply at that stage of the war. The one time a German plane did dive on their balloon, it was not to blast them out of the sky; instead, the curious pilot merely swooped in for a closer look at the painting that an artist had emblazoned on the silk skin of the balloon—an angry elephant stomping on a hapless worm.

While serving in Europe, Matt Griswold developed a very close friendship with a gallant, young French officer. Such close personal bonds are one of the key motivators that military members use to unite them in solidarity against their common enemies. Unfortunately, this particular bond did not last beyond wartime. A few years after hostilities ended, Dr. Matt visited France. Although he hadn't kept up a correspondence with his comrade in arms, he certainly expected that their friendship forged in fire would be a lifetime alliance. Alas, he dropped in on his friend, in Brittany, only to be rebuffed and shown the door in a rude and hasty manner. Apparently, the mood after the war in France had turned decidedly anti-American, and this had colored his friend's attitude toward all Americans. Matt was doubly hurt. The loss of a good friend was difficult to bear, but the ingratitude of the French after the military efforts that the United States made to save their country was not at all palatable.

Dr. Matt returned from his overseas adventures and, like his progenitor, Matthew VI, took up the study of medicine. Unlike his ancestor, though, Dr. Matt completed his academic program and entered into practice in Old Lyme. Not only was he a major contributor to the good health of its citizens, but he also took an active role in maintaining the civic and cultural well-being of the community. Dr. Matt was instrumental in several projects that benefited the town, including moving the post office and shopping center so as to preserve the pristine small-town character of Lyme Street. He was also involved in the creation of the Florence Griswold Museum and provided several works of art to its collections. Dr. Matt was a proud member and supporter of the Congregational Church. He was also one of the original members of the Old Lyme Beach Club, a mainstay of the town's social network.

Chapter 17

FINE FURNITURE, LIBERTY SHIPS, PUBLIC SERVICE AND PHILANTHROPY

While one loop of the Griswold family was busily making the skillets to cook our country's steak and eggs, another was busy making the tables and chairs so that Americans could sit down and eat them. Through school connections and marriage, Bill and John Griswold rose to top management positions with the W&J Sloane Company, one of the premier manufacturers, wholesalers and retailers of fine commercial and residential furnishings. Yale educated, with advanced degrees from the Harvard Business School, the brothers learned every aspect of the business from the ground up and became experts in every aspect of interior design.

An interesting turn in that career path occurred with the coming of World War II, when government officials convinced John that his knowledge and skills would be of best use to his country in designing and crafting the interior spaces of Liberty ships. Liberty ships were key factors in the Allied victory in the war. At 442 feet long and 56 feet wide, they drew 27 feet, were powered with 2,500-horsepower engines and could cruise at eleven knots. During the course of the war, they carried millions of tons of munitions and equipment and hundreds of thousands of soldiers, sailors and airmen across the world's oceans. They were a linchpin in the production process that allowed the Allies to overwhelm the Axis with material and personnel.

The Sloane Company had previous experience in fitting out passenger and commercial vessels. Among the important ships it furnished were the elegant ocean liners *America* and the *United States*. This experience gave John a leg up when it came to establishing the policies, procedures and logistics

Bill Griswold during his role as president of the W&J Sloane Furniture Company. *Griswold family archives.*

necessary to make these workhorses of the oceans livable. The North Carolina shipyard that he helped to build produced 243 vessels during the course of the war. Of these, 28 were lost in action, but none to mechanical or structural failure.

The exigencies of turning out ships at breakneck speed during wartime made for some innovative production strategies and a few hair-raising moments. John instituted a system he called team production, which was essentially an assembly line on a very large scale. Men and women ran from ship to ship doing one task over and over again. Choosing the right foremen to keep this system up and running was a huge managerial challenge. John developed a system that allowed him to personally observe all three of the eight-hour shifts that were his responsibility. Staggering naps and with the help of lots of coffee, he was able to keep the wheels of production rolling smoothly.

There was adventure and humor associated with the job, too. On one occasion, as they were taking a ship out for its initial sea trials, the crew tested the antiaircraft guns with several fusillades. Since it was a foggy, misty morning, they neglected to see the blimp that was on antisubmarine patrol high above them. Some choice words were passed from sky to sea on that Carolina morning. On a more humorous note, since the wartime supply of jeeps was scarce, the Coast Guardsmen patrolling the beaches looking for submarines were issued horses that the military purchased from local farms. Sailors on horseback are not always pretty sights, and one brave mariner was thrown from his horse. He sat on the beach as he saw the animal splash into the water. An outgoing tide swept the horse seaward, where another Coastie reported it as being an enemy submarine! All ended well, however. The horse was rescued, the Coast Guard had a new butt for endless jokes and the *New York Times* had a story to place smiles on readers' faces in the midst of grim war news.

John and Bill's brother Dwight followed the family path that led to the healing arts. After his graduation from Yale, he went to the Columbia Presbyterian College of Physicians and Surgeons. During the war, he was stationed at the Walter Reed Army Hospital in Washington, D.C. Caring for wounded service men was an exhausting job, and Dwight developed a work ethic that demanded lots of hours and very little sleep. After the war, he brought that work ethic to civilian practice on the polio floors of McCook General Hospital in Hartford, Connecticut. Unfortunately, Dwight contracted a case of lumbar polio, the very worst form of the crippling disease that killed thousands yearly before a vaccine was discovered. He died within a week of its onset. His best friend and colleague at the hospital believed that he developed the disease because of fatigue brought about by the demanding work schedule he imposed on himself.

After the war, John enrolled in the Pratt Institute to further his knowledge of design and artistic techniques. He put together a research facility that became a laboratory for the design and development of new products and

Dwight Griswold in his World War II uniform. *Griswold family archives.*

was backed by several of the largest corporations in the country at the time. His group sponsored a lecture by Buckminster Fuller, the always interesting futurist. When Fuller asked Griswold how long he wanted him to speak for, Griswold replied, "I don't know, we have a lot of time." It was the wrong answer. Fuller went on full throttle for over two and a half hours, but his material was so relevant and his delivery style so peppy that no one in the audience yawned even once.

John went on to found a few other companies dedicated to the design of superior commercial space, including the office of the chairman of RCA. He also designed the New England States Building for the 1964 World's Fair, the Man and His Health Pavilion at Montreal's Expo in 1967 and the Encyclopedia Britannica Exhibit at the World's Fair held in Osaka, Japan, in 1970.

After touring the world on the fair circuit, Griswold returned to Connecticut, where he shuffled back and forth between Greenwich and Old Lyme. At this stage of his life, he became devoted to philanthropic activities and causes. The list of organizations that benefit from his time, energy and resources is a long one and includes the Berzelius Senior Society; the Greenwich Country Day School; Christ Church in Greenwich; the International College in Beirut, Lebanon; the Boys Clubs of America; and the Children's Aid Society. During this period, John was able to devote more time to his growing family. He also was able to wrap his hands around the tillers of several sailboats, including his beloved *Sadie*. More time for golf was also a plus.

John's brother Bill served as president and treasurer of the W&J Sloane Company. He left his positions there after the company underwent a corporate reshuffling in the early 1950s. He eventually moved the middle of the country, accepting highest-level management offices for General Mills, and, later, New York, where he worked for Lever Brothers. After returning to Connecticut, he also immersed himself in philanthropy. He focused on Old Lyme, becoming active in many local organizations, including the Florence Griswold Museum. He played an important role in the development of the MacCurdy-Salisbury Education Fund, whose purpose is to provide financial assistance to Old Lyme students as they pursue four-year degree programs at the colleges of their choice. Currently, the fund has an endowment of $6 million and provides assistance to over one hundred local students. Bill's sons carry on the family themes of medicine, government, military service and commerce.

Chapter 18

THE TWENTIETH CENTURY
AND BEYOND

SLOANE PURSUES A CAREER IN THE MILITARY

In keeping with family tradition, Bill's son Sloane pursued a career in the military. He sums it up in his own words:

It all began after a failed semester at Yale University, a week completely in the doghouse at home and an enlistment in the army. That was followed with basic training at Ft. Carson, Colorado, and in the summer of 1956, I boarded a troop ship for the ten-day trip across the pond. I was a radio repairman, qualified to change fuses and tubes, and we ended up in Ulm, Germany, just south of Stuttgart.

Life was a parade of field duty, maneuvers, cleaning all the gear and vehicles and sampling the best beer in the world. Our unit of the 8th Infantry Division moved to Sandhofen, just outside of Mannheim, where we did more of the same. Along the way, I acquired a wife who fortunately spoke English, three stepsons and two daughters. With a couple bumps, I made sergeant and in 1960 was transferred back to the States, headed to Ft. Sam Houston in San Antonio, TX.

The trip was an adventure—visas for all, passports and a prop-engine plane landing in NJ. Dad met us with a wagon, and we had three weeks in Old Lyme at 100 Acres cabins. The weeklong trip to Texas was also an adventure. [It was] before interstates, and [we drove] a small sports car and brother Douglas's clunker, which [later] sold for scrap.

Texas was super hot in mid-July—we learned about air conditioners quickly. I was in a signal company and had more maneuvers and cleaning stuff. An ex-navy pilot in the company persuaded me to apply for Officer Candidate School, since my job was headed into a dead-end alley. I was accepted and journeyed to Fort Benning School for Boys. Six months of double timing, shining boots, spit-shining floors, square meals and running the gamut of infantry weapons, plus more maneuvers, spit out a brand-new second lieutenant in June of 1962.

Orders came for me to return to Ft. Carson, with a nine-week stop in Ft. Knox, KY, so I could become an armor officer. All this involved moving with family, packing household goods and seeing the countryside. After checking in at Ft. Carson, someone told me that no, I was going to Camp Wolters outside of Ft. Worth, TX, for flight training. After unloading, [it was] back in the car and off to the next adventure.

Flying a helicopter was major FUN. [It was] difficult at first (we lost about a third of our class in the pre-solo stage), but it was fun. I was in a special Tiger class, learning to shoot machine guns from the helicopter and adjusting artillery, up at Ft. Sill, OK. Soon I had some nice silver wings on my chest and was told to head back to Ft. Carson. After the first chapter, we sat in a motel until I learned that we belonged in Ft. Rucker, AL. [Then it was] back in the car for another trip, checking in with the Tactics Department at Rucker. Along the way, son Bill was born in Texas, and Sarah showed up in Alabama.

My jobs were teaching survival to pilots, who started coming in numbers as the demand in Vietnam rose. In 1965, it was my turn to go to Southeast Asia, which I did. I ended up in Pleiku in the central highlands. Three weeks into the tour, the Viet Cong decided to shell our camp. One round hit the "hooch" I was in, and I ended up with a broken leg, a bunch of holes and a trip to Clark AFB in the Philippines, where they attached a cast. Several long flights brought me back to San Antonio to Brooke Army Hospital, and five months of that healed the leg. I pleaded to be sent back to Ft. Rucker, where the family was, but no, it was Ft. Meade, MD, and an armored cavalry unit. [After] six months there, mostly flying logistics-type missions, I learned the unit was being assigned to the 1st Air Cav Division headed to Vietnam. So, after buying our first house in MD, we pulled up stakes and set out for Ft. Rucker, [where I would be] a flight instructor. As an officer, that totals eight moves in a little over three years. Then a friend's dad told me about the fact that the Coast Guard was looking for military aviators. Did I jump? You bet. I did attain my first captaincy as an Army O-3.

In June of 1967, I bid farewell to the army, and we traveled to Elizabeth City, NC, and the Coast Guard air station there, where I was Lieutenant Junior Grade (O-2). We bought our second house, and I learned how to fly instruments and even went to Mobile, AL, for transition into the HU-16E Grumman Albatross, or "Goat," as we called it. A big twin-prop amphibious plane, I learned to land it on the water, anchor it and pick up a mooring—neat stuff. It also enabled me to learn about LORAN (long range navigation) and fly as a navigator on the C-130, a four-turbine-engine cargo plane. That took me to places in Mexico, Argentina, Canada and points in between on search and rescue missions. My main job was helicopters, and the Sikorsky HH-52A was the helo of choice. Search and rescue was serious FUN. Pulling someone out of a bad situation was ever more satisfying than practicing for Vietnam.

After two years, I was assigned to the icebreaker section in Mobile, where we stood up detachments to join a Coast Guard icebreaker headed to the poles. My first trip was aboard CGC *Edisto* out of Boston. Here was a whole new dimension, flying off a 269-foot vessel and tucking two helicopters into a tiny hangar while folding blades and traveling with four officers and eleven enlisted men. We were headed to Antarctica, with stops at the Panama Canal; Tahiti; Auckland, New Zealand; and McMurdo station on the Antarctic continent. After six months with a one-month sojourn in Wellington, NZ (the ship broke its rudder and needed a dry dock), we headed home. The navy helos were out of commission in McMurdo, so we flew many of the scientific missions they would have. I learned a great deal about the continent and captured a ride on a navy C-130 to South Pole Station, 10,000 feet above sea level on an 8,000-foot slab of ice that is slowly moving.

After a summer back home in Mobile, with camping and water skiing, [it was] back to the CGC Burton Island out of Long Beach, CA, for a return to the frozen continent. We slid down the west coast of South America, stopping in Lima, Peru, and Punta Arenas, Chile. We visited Palmer station and then sailed to McMurdo. Unfortunately, nothing broke, so we spent another six months deployed. When we got back again, we had orders for Air Station, Miami, the busiest search and rescue station in the country.

Every fourth day, we had the 24-hour "duty" living aboard the station. The station was very busy. We had great challenges looking for missing boaters, saving some and notably assisting with the Eastern Air Lines 1011 crash in the Everglades just before New Year's Eve. I transitioned back in to the HU-16E and had a few trips down in the Caribbean, visiting some of the islands that only tourists get to see. At times, we launched so quickly that we had only our flight suits and maybe a toilet kit.

From there, I was divorced and married Sam and was transferred to Mobile and the SAR Division, flying fixed wing. The venerable Goats were being retired, and we transitioned to the C-131, basically a Convair 240, twin-engine, pressurized 200-knot aircraft. This plane had legs and allowed us to venture even farther afield. After three years there, in 1978, we got orders to proceed to Kodiak Island, Alaska. Back into the Sikorsky helicopter, flying off 278-foot cutters in the Bering enforcing the new 200-mile economic zone on commercial fisheries. Not only did we fly off the cutters, sometimes in foul weather, but we also became adept members of the boarding teams that went aboard fishing vessels from China, Taiwan, Poland, USSR, Japan and South Korea. The communist vessels rarely disobeyed the rules, but the others played cat-and-mouse. We devised all sorts of tactics to try and catch them in no-fish areas and even took an army soldier from Korea to listen to the crew jest about a second set of books. The Soviets offered us caviar and vodka, but the return to the ship down a rope ladder to a plunging motor surf boat kept us all sober. In 1980, I was promoted to commander, and my flying days were over. Our next station was Juneau, Alaska, 17th District Headquarters. While Sam was unhappy about another Alaska tour, I eagerly moved into the Military Readiness job. There, I worked on war plans, learned a whole new vocabulary and played war games with JTF Alaska, a combined army/ air force command in Anchorage. I teamed up with a navy commander from CINCPAC, the overall command for the entire Pacific region. We introduced naval problems into the basically land-based scenarios and enjoyed the experience. After three years at this, and because our youngest daughter was becoming a senior in high school, I moved to the Boating Safety arena, becoming the director of the CG Auxiliary.

Here, I learned about the CG's mission in recreational boating safety, as well as managing 450 or so Auxiliary volunteers. These folks offered their time and private boats, planes and radios to the Coast Guard, teaching boating classes, examining citizens' boats and performing patrols for the Coast Guard. It also entailed many trips around the state, visiting flotillas in the towns and cities around the coast. Obviously, I was having too much fun, so within a year, my boss reassigned me to the Personnel Division.

Knowing nothing about personnel, we immediately launched into a huge reorganization combining Yeomen with Storekeepers, bringing the financial functions into Personnel. I also had the medical folks, training budgets and civilian personnel to contend with. This two-year job was made ever so much easier having two senior enlisted people and a Chief Warrant Officer to deal with the nuts and bolts. We pulled the division out of a pit of trouble, and I attribute our performance to the good report cards that enabled me to be selected for my second captaincy (O-6).

Two years of this finally led us to the point of leaving Alaska after eight years. Our next stop was Governor's Island off the tip of Manhattan. Talk about culture shock. Getting on or off the island involved a ferry boat ride, and suddenly we were thrust onto the East Side Drive with thousands of kamikaze drivers. Soon we were enjoying this tour. I was again back as the director of Auxiliary for the 3rd District, which encompassed CT, NY, NJ and a lot of PA, with two regions. From 450 volunteers, we had about 5,000, and thankfully I had experienced a year of that in Alaska. In 1986, the Coast Guard reorganized—I think a repeated cycle—and the 3rd District was to be no more. My job was split between Boston and Portsmouth, VA. Therefore, I was transferred to the Captain's Graveyard, Headquarters, Washington, D.C.

We bought five acres outside of Falling Waters, WV, and I began commuting on a train into Washington. The two-hour-plus commute involved the train, D.C.'s metro and a bus ride. For the next six years, I was the chief director, Auxiliary, and was immersed in the recreational boating mission. I got involved with all the alphabet-soup organizations of boating, traveled to countless conferences all over the country and put my membership in the Auxiliary on hold until I retired in 1993, with 37 years of active service. My retirement was aboard an Auxiliary facility (pleasure boat) moored in a marina next to the Headquarters building. My family was aboard, my Admiral and I were in dress whites with swords and afterwards we had a lovely reception first at the Fort McNair Officers' Club and, later, at our place in Falling Waters.

I had a very rewarding career, got much further than I ever thought I would, made some lifelong friends and have maintained my presence in the boating safety world through the CG Auxiliary. I think I covered the waterfront.

Peter Goes into International Business

Sloane's brother Peter followed in the family's business tradition.

Growing up on Wyndhurst Farm, Griswold Point, in the footsteps of many generations dating back to 1640, forged incredible experiences, memories and lessons learned. While my three brothers and I enjoyed more than our share of opportunity and privilege, we worked hard with the farm hands, who taught us life-long lessons as well as some fairly colorful language for our age. Besides weeding, taking care of the animals and learning how to drive trucks and tractors and helping with the haying, our labors generated tangible results.

Instead of receiving an allowance each week, we were paid five cents an hour at first with raises that eventually made it all the way up to twenty-five cents. Our earnings had to last for the entire school year. Paying for a movie quickly became a calculation of how many working hours the ticket represented. Learning the value of money and earning our own way instilled an appreciation for hard work and being thrifty. While classmates were able to afford comic books, popcorn and whatever they desired, I preferred to save my money, placing it in a bank savings account.

Every family activity and major celebration on Griswold Point involved not just my immediate family, but also many of my cousins and multiple generations of elders. Everyone participated in the Fourth of July celebration, the highlight being our very own splendid parade with costumes and homemade floats, followed by a potluck feast complete with ice cream and, finally, speeches covering interesting topics. Then the games would begin, first with the children and then all the adults would join in. [It was] great fun for everyone.

On Griswold Point, old buildings, antique furniture and paintings, not to mention ancient farm implements, surrounded us. We often heard stories about how our early relatives first settled in Old Lyme. They were masons, attorneys, inventors, manufacturers, retailers and politicians. I always liked the tales about how George Griswold and Nathanial Lane formed a shipping company during the early 1800s, trading with China. Their initials, G.G. and N.L., became the firm's motto: "Great Gains, No Losses."

Many relatives lived overseas and traveled extensively. As children, their stories expanded our horizons, providing glimpses of how others lived

around the world. One uncle even made a major discovery of an ancient city in Peru. Another built railroads in the Pacific Northwest. And yet, most of them always returned to Old Lyme for vacations and to live here in retirement. While the family heritage tended to overwhelm new spouses, everyone got along with one other, a remarkable achievement.

The family cherishes numerous traditions, with each generation expanding the amazing antics. One tradition involves temporarily kidnapping the groom during the reception, who must then be rescued by the bride before the newlyweds can depart on their honeymoon. My own wedding did not escape the clutch of clever tactics, horrifying my new mother-in-law. The retelling of these famous incidents is cause for much hilarity among family members and only deepens the desire to continue the tradition.

Being expected at a young age to learn how to relate to all of the relatives, young and old, and to make intelligent conversation with adults, honed my interpersonal skills. As the third son, I was often the intermediary between my two oldest brothers, Sloane and Douglas, who fought continuously. Understandably, a talent for diplomacy and an ability to converse with anyone became important skills later in life.

During college, I was a history major but then focused on international business in graduate school. I joined the oldest bank in Boston and enjoyed numerous assignments during a long career, including four overseas positions in Argentine, Venezuela, the Dominican Republic and Canada. I often thought about my relatives who accomplished similar challenges. Knowing their achievements provided me with a high level of self-confidence, energy and a desire to succeed. Establishing rapport with prospects and difficult clients was relatively easy for me. I think my extended family trained me well.

After retirement, I became a career coach assisting clients searching for new challenges and opportunities. I developed a method enabling clients to determine their own passion. Once identified, they were eager to undertake a focused search resulting in a successful transition.

Opposite, top: A photo of what appears to be a water tower in the early twentieth century (though there is some debate as to its function and provenance). *Griswold family archives.*

Opposite, bottom: This twentieth-century boating scene (oil on canvas) was painted from a family photograph by Frederick Schavoir. *Photo by author.*

William Chadwick's painting entitled *Bathers on Griswold Beach*. Note the rock on the shoreline, which is now a few hundred feet offshore. *Courtesy of the Florence Griswold Museum.*

My two surviving bothers, Sloane and Timothy, and I inherited our parents' home and farm on Griswold Point, known as The Big House, which had been built in 1840. Our challenge was to manage this property so that we would be able to pass it on to the next generation. After my father's death, we introduced an annual Family Reunion Week whereby all of my nephews and nieces and their families would congregate on the Point to undertake numerous projects designed to maintain and improve this property. We three brothers were determined to share our deep affection for the Point as well as convey a sense of stewardship to the next generation for what they would inherit someday.

Collectively, we tackle very difficult challenges. Everyone participates and contributes their own skills ranging from building sheds, restoring an old house, repairing structural beams, pouring concrete, replacing roofs, painting, landscaping and kitchen duty. Most importantly, we all have fun and get to know one another better each year.

While we collectively are determined to preserve this precious property, the reality of real estate taxes is fast becoming an insurmountable challenge.

All of the individual families who live on the Point have joined together to create the Griswold Point Association, enabling us to collectively compare and explore ideas to meet the challenges we face. This Association has brought the extended family even closer together. More than ever, we are determined to preserve the Point for future generations.

DOUGLAS BECOMES A MEDICAL MAN

Douglas Griswold, an orthopedic surgeon, thanks his military service for providing him with a great deal of on-the-job training and hands-on experience during the Vietnam War. Doug did his undergraduate work at Yale, where he rowed on the crew team, wrestled and was captain of the football team. Continuing the family tradition, he sang with the Whiffenpoofs, but he turned down an invitation to join the Skull and Bones in order to focus on his studies. He was inspired to pursue a medical career when, as a boy, he watched in wonder as his uncle Dr. Dwight Griswold dissected a groundhog and provided a tutorial narrative as the process unfolded. He went to medical school at Boston University. After completing his military service, he joined the staff at Windham Hospital, where he partnered with the fellow who took care of the UCONN men's basketball team. Douglas's ability to mend broken bones and heal patients became legendary. The mother of a child who was suffering from back pain called Doug from New York City after several fruitless visits to other doctors. Doug listened intently to the mother and then suggested what should be done. The mother told Doug's family many years later how his suggestions over the phone saved her daughter's life. Doug became chief of staff at Windham Hospital before his untimely death.

TIMOTHY THE POLITICIAN

Timothy Griswold followed his brother Peter into the banking world, working at several banks in the Hartford area. However, this was at a time when the friendly neighborhood banks were beginning to transform into the

Timothy Griswold continued the family tradition of public service with his bid for first selectman of Old Lyme in 1997. *Courtesy of Emily Griswold.*

A grateful community recognized Tim Griswold's service to the town. *Courtesy of Emily Griswold.*

bigger, less friendly regional and national banks. Tim was not fond of the dehumanizing, strictly-by-the-numbers direction that banking was taking as it became increasingly computerized. He decided to make a career change and devote himself to a life of public service and governance like many of his Griswold ancestors before him.

He made a successful run and was elected Old Lyme's first selectman in 1996, serving in that capacity for fourteen years. As first selectman of Old Lyme, he had to deal with issues faced by many other towns, including the education budget and senior services. He oversaw major school renovation projects and was instrumental in the creation of the senior center. His domain covered twenty-seven square miles but offered some demographic challenges as its population doubled every summer and then shrank back to a fairly stable number during the winter months. The swollen summer population often included revelers lured to town by the public beach and its popular beer halls. It posed challenges to a six-man town police force and its lone resident state trooper.

The seasonal nature of the town is reflected in its zoning. Some areas do not permit bars or package stores. The prevalence of summer cottages presented Tim with lots of headaches and challenges in terms of sewage and water issues. The state and town became involved in a political wrestling match regarding sewer and septic issues. One issue that Tim had to deal with was the town's proximity to the Millstone Nuclear Power Station. Plans regarding possible hazards ranged from the distribution of potassium iodine pills to what the contingency plans were in case of a full-blown meltdown. The severe weather events that occurred on his watch also provided their share of challenges and adventures. Tim continues to serve on many town boards, commissions and committees. Most notably, in terms of this project, he is the chair of the Old Lyme Historical Society. He also looks after the day-to-day operations of Griswold Point in terms of maintenance, event planning and overall operations. He shares administrative functions with his brothers.

Chapter 19

FARMS, FLOWERS AND FISH

Since it was settled in the 1640s, Griswold Point has been a self-sustaining source of food, forage, fish, flowers and cottage industries, including bookbinding. When Matthew I received his original land grant from George Fenwick and the English noblemen, it included farmland not only at the mouth of the river but also in several inland areas. Salt hay was, by happy circumstance of nature, the first crop to be harvested. But the cultivation of corn, wheat, rye and other grains soon followed. Orchards were planted to provide fruit for export and the basic ingredients for cider, brandies and other spirituous staples.

Even though they were engaged in public service, educational and legal pursuits, the denizens of the point continued to improve and enhance the land. Houses, barns, outbuildings, greenhouses, windmills and water towers sprang up to increase the yield of the territory. Cattle, horses, oxen, goats, chickens and other farm animals provided meat, tallow, eggs, bone meal and plow-pulling power. In the 1930s, Griswold Point was famous for its sheep-shearing competitions. Old photographs show dozens of men lined up with their sheep trussed to metal restraints, hoping to be the fastest cutters of the most wool.

Matthew Griswold VI had hoped to devote himself to a life practicing the medical arts, but the early death of his parents compelled him to give up his studies and take up farming and fishing full time to provide for his siblings and extended family. Fishing was what he truly loved, and he was very good at it. Griswold Point is particularly blessed in that it is the place where, each spring,

The lane looking toward Long Island Sound. Elm trees formed an arch. *Griswold family archives.*

shad return to the mouth of the Connecticut River to swim upstream and spawn. This means that the fishermen who set their nets and weirs as close to the sound as possible have the first and best crack at the delectable fish.

For centuries, Connecticut River shad have been prized for their sweet taste and good protein. They can be cooked, salted, pickled or smoked,

The hurricane of 1938 made landfall not far from Griswold Point. *Griswold family archives.*

making them a year-round staple. The Indians and early colonists also used them as fertilizer for the crops that sustained them. The downside of shad is their intricate network of over 1,200 bones. The indigenous people referred to them as "inside-out porcupines" because of their numerous, sharp bones. Up to the current era, although the commercial shad fishery is barely sputtering along, boning shad has traditionally been a gender-specific task relegated to women. It is a skill still passed down from mother to daughter.

The women of Matthew VI's time must have been well skilled in its mysteries because Matthew VI caught a whole lot of shad. The season runs only from April to June, and shad can be captured only at night because they can see nets during the day. So for the spring months, Matthew didn't get much sleep. He built a series of docks and piers on the river to accommodate his boats and nets. He rigged his dock with a large gun, which he fired off every time he landed one thousand shad. The gun was often heard several times a night. Griswold shipped his shad by boat and wagon up and down the river and sound.

Shad was not the only product exported by the Griswolds. Beginning in the nineteenth century and lasting well into the beginning of the twentieth, "the Aunties" developed a large greenhouse operation that raised

At the turn of the twentieth century, carnations were grown at the point and shipped to New York via ferry and rail. *Griswold family archives.*

Griswold Point continues its tradition of growing beautiful flowers. *Author's collection.*

thousands of carnations, which they then shipped by train for the New York and Philadelphia markets. The seven Aunties, four of whom remained unmarried, lived in the Governor Roger Griswold house and entertained grandly and often. Family lore has several favorite Auntie tales. A favorite of Matthew X details how his father and a Yale classmate were dragooned into paddling a canoe with a rather large Auntie as a passenger up the Lieutenant River to Miss Florence Griswold's museum. They accomplished this feat with much cussing under their breath and some help from an incoming tide. But when it came time to paddle her back, the tide was still coming in and her crew mutinied, requiring that she call for an automobile to convey her back to the point.

Another Auntie story is not quite so light-hearted. It seems that when a huge gale blew up around 1910, an unlucky fisherman from the Fair Haven section of New Haven had his boat blown ashore in front of the Aunties' house. They rushed to the beach to find him suffering from hypothermia, badly bruised and generally confused. They carried him to the house, gave him tea and brandy and ensconced him on the sofa under copious quilts. The next day, he was much better but stated that another day of recuperation might be just the ticket. The next morning, the Aunties awoke to find him long gone—along with all of their very precious silver! They dispatched riders in all directions and found him waiting to cross the Connecticut River at the Chester Ferry. The Aunties got their silver back and agreed to the truism that no good deed goes unpunished.

Another Auntie had a small building put up just north of the greenhouses and turned it into a bookbindery. Though none of the books that it produced can be found, it was a rare instance that a product of the point was not animal or vegetable. Today, the point still furnishes hay to local horse farms. Its most recent commercial manifestation, however, has been the development of Judge's Farm. Originally started as a Christmas tree–growing operation, it has morphed into a solar-powered, primarily organic wholesale flower farm that grows thousands of annuals and perennials for garden centers up and down the East Coast. The spirit of the Aunties lives on in the truckloads of blossoms that roll out of Old Lyme every day, destined to grace the gardens of homes and businesses.

Chapter 20

THE GRIS

In 1776, when Sala (sometimes spelled Selah) Griswold built his tavern on Main Street in Essex, it was the first three-story building to be erected in Connecticut. It still stands today as a happy hearth of hospitality, famous for its fine food, warming spirits, maritime art and artifacts and welcoming guest rooms. The Griswold House, also called the Griswold Inn or, these days, simply "The Gris," has played several important roles in the history of the Connecticut River Estuary. It has maintained its dedication to that history. It houses an extraordinary collection of paintings, photographs and memorabilia that catalogue the region's sea-faring experience from the days of the founding fathers and mothers through the present. It also hosts events that commemorate the history of Essex and the music that sailors sung as they hoisted sails and toiled around capstans.

Even before the Revolutionary War, Essex was an important shipbuilding center that produced sloops, schooners and square-rigged ships that took Connecticut's produce, provender, lumber, horses and cattle to the Caribbean and Europe. The Griswold family began building, captaining and managing ships in the area in the early seventeenth century. But it was during the War for Independence that Essex produced its most famous vessel, the *Oliver Cromwell*. The *Cromwell* was full rigged and proved to be a thorn in the side of the Royal Navy. It captured nine British ships before it was finally taken and forced to sail under the enemy's flag.

The Essex area also spawned the most interesting vessel of the Revolution, David Bushnell's *Turtle*, arguably the world's first naval submarine. Skeptics

When Sala Griswold built his tavern, Essex was sending privateers down the river to harass British shipping. *Author's collection.*

scoffed at the idea, but Bushnell had made believers out of key national political and naval luminaries. At a critical juncture in the *Turtle*'s construction, Bushnell's funding ran out. The governor of Connecticut and the Legislative Council of Safety appropriated sixty pounds of emergency money to see the project to completion. It was Lieutenant Matthew Griswold who was charged with the responsibility of making the trip to Lebanon to retrieve the funds. He did so, and the *Turtle* was completed. Although it was less than a success in sinking enemy ships, it truly provided the inspiration for the fleets of undersea vessels that slip under the surface of all the world's seas today. An excellently crafted replica of the *Turtle* can be seen at the Connecticut River Museum, just down the street from the Griswold Inn.

It was during the War of 1812 that Essex and the Griswold Inn played significant roles. On the night of April 7, 1814, British sailors and marines, under cover of darkness, rowed upriver to the town and set fire to more than two dozen ships that were moored in the harbor or under construction.

The British were in possession of first-rate intelligence regarding ships' positions and local defenses provided to them by a traitor to the American cause. Two Griswold-built ships were among the victims—an eighteen-gun privateer and a sixteen-gun vessel that had yet to be christened. It was the most devastating attack on U.S. soil and water until it was eclipsed by Pearl Harbor. The British slipped back down the river with a quantity of Essex rum among their prizes.

Recently, diligent new research has called for a reassessment of the raid. Scholars aver that the narrative should be changed to reflect what actually occurred. In the traditional telling, the traitor was a either a jilted lover or a Freemason of the same lodge as the British commander. The men of Essex were said to have crowded into the taproom of the Griswold Inn and consumed large quantities of spirituous libations while the enemy ravaged their boats and stole their rum. In fact, the annual parade that marks the event is traditionally called Loser's Day. New scholarship, however, suggests that the Essex men put up resistance and that the British came under cannon fire from both sides of the river as they made their way back to their ships.

The Griswold Inn also found itself in another battle, the War Between the Wets and the Dries. In the early nineteenth century, backed by women across the country, a burgeoning temperance movement took root and stubbornly accrued legislative and moral power. Protests against establishments that served alcohol became commonplace, and many so-called watering holes surrendered and really did become watering holes. The Griswold Inn became a "temperance hotel" for a brief interlude, but soon enough its taproom rang with convivial laughter as the ale flowed once again. There are still some temperance banners to be seen among the inn's decorations.

The temperance movement reached its apogee with the implementation of the Eighteenth Amendment, which brought about Prohibition. But the Griswold Inn didn't let a little thing like federal law stanch the flow of its popular potables. Despite frequent raids by revenuers, the Gris managed to keep the whistles of its patrons wet. This was due, in part, to the excellent opportunities that the inlets and coves of Essex provided to smugglers. Fast motorboats would rendezvous with mother ships full of hooch on Rum Row, beyond the three-mile limit at sea, and zoom their illicit cargo up the river under cover of fog and darkness. Some of that cargo found its way into the time-honored taproom of the Griswold Inn.

Much to the relief of many, Prohibition was eventually repealed, and the outlaw cachet associated with cocktails at the Gris was replaced with the bonhomie of a nicely fashioned potable in anticipation of a delicious

The Griswold Inn, circa 1860, a few years after it was known as a "temperance hotel." *Courtesy of the Connecticut Historical Society.*

Today, the Griswold Inn remains a source of fine food and grog. *Author's collection.*

The sloop *Saloola*, built in Essex, sailing off Griswold Point. Oil on canvas by Frederick Schavoir. *Photo by author.*

meal. The inn evolved throughout the twentieth century, keeping pace with culinary trends while retaining traditional fare on its menus, such as Connecticut River shad and roe. In the twenty-first century, the Griswold Inn is an internationally famous destination whose charm, character and cuisine are celebrated by customers and guests from all over the world.

Essex retains its maritime heritage as well. It is a famous yachting center, the home port of many sailing and power vessels. It is a must-visit port of call on the itineraries of those cruising New England waters. Its harbor is home to the Connecticut River Museum and the Essex Boat Works. Craftsmen still create the occasional custom sailboat. Griswold family members still sail *Saloola*, a twenty-foot wooden sloop built in Essex in the middle of the twentieth century. A visit to Essex, whether by land or water, provides the opportunity to enjoy a delectable lunch or dinner at the Gris.

Chapter 21

POINTING TO THE FUTURE

As Heraclitus said a couple thousand years ago, "Only change is permanent." Griswold Point has seen its share of changes in the past four hundred years. It has weathered social, cultural and political vicissitudes and has come through with flying colors. Placed within the context of its vulnerability as a spit of sand standing against a rising ocean, the future of the point will be increasingly influenced by environmental factors that are affecting it at an increasing rate. This focus on the environment was predicted decades ago by Evan Griswold, and it is of ongoing concern to him today.

Evan is the premier environmentalist who resides at Griswold Point. He has been involved with the Nature Conservancy since its inception in Connecticut. His efforts to preserve and maintain the environmental quality of the point and its flora and fauna stretch back to his earliest years. Forty years ago, he wrote, "The ecological significance of the [Griswold Point] preserve is its protection of the vitally important estuary and salt marshes inland from it, as well as its uniqueness as an example of undisturbed beach/marsh ecosystem. It is among the few such ecosystems remaining on the entire northeast coast." The same concerns that he voiced back then are still prominent today.

Interestingly, in his report, "An Ecological Inventory of Griswold Point Preserve," he cites the most pressing environmental problem on the point as being the preponderance of tenters, who set up makeshift dwellings during the summer months to fish both recreationally and commercially. Camping on Griswold Point lasted for much of the twentieth century. Some campers returned every year for decades. But as plastic boat manufacturing made small boats more affordable and easier to handle, day-trippers increasingly competed for space with the tenters, and litter and vandalism became increasing problems. Tenting, as per Evan's strong recommendation, was finally eliminated in the 1980s.

Today, the Nature Conservancy and the Audubon Society send plover wardens to the point during the summer to track the nesting and breeding activities of piping plovers and least terns. The habitat available to these birds has decreased considerably in the past few years due to beach erosion, storm surges and rising water levels. Because it is such a unique and delicate part of the region's ecosystem, the point is a bellwether of environmental change in a time when such changes are of increasing global concern.

Global concerns notwithstanding, the future generations who will enjoy Griswold Point will have new sets of challenges we have not yet had to face and overcome. They will do this, however, with a sense of place and people that has endured for almost four centuries. It is this connection rooted in history but continually moving forward that makes the human adventure the exciting journey that it always has been and always will be.

Adeline Bartlett Allyn, in her conclusion to *Black Hall Traditions and Reminiscences*, sums up the relationship between people and place beautifully: "Black Hall sustains its ancient natural beauties. The ripple of waves can still be heard on the beach; the soft skies hang over the charming scene; the radiant sunset delights the eye with marvelous afterglow; the moonlight shimmers on the silvery waves as it has since so long ago…the sweet spirit of hospitality, family, affection…May we feel the inspiration of the past as it lingers in this beloved spot, to keep before us the ideals of all these brave, noble and courteous gentlefolks who lived 'bravely and swiftly.'"

SELECTED SOURCES

Abbot, Katherine. *Old Paths and Legends of the New England Border.* New York: Knickerbocker Press, 1909.

Allyn, Adeline Bartlett. *Black Hall Traditions and Reminiscences.* Hartford, CT: Case, Lockwood & Brainard, 1908.

Banks, John. *Connecticut Yankees at Antietam.* Charleston, SC: The History Press, 2013.

Barret, Walter. *Old Merchants of New York City.* New York: Thomas R. Knox and Co., 1863.

Coe, Sophia Fidelia Hale. *Memoranda Relating to the Ancestry of Sophia Fidelia Hall.* Meriden, CT: Curtiss-Way Co., 1902.

Connecticut Supreme Court. *Proceedings of the Connecticut Supreme Court.* Vol. 62. Hartford, CT: Connecticut Supreme Court, 1884.

Day, Bonnie, and James Wells Griswold. *Our Griswold Family in England Before 1639.* Exeter, NH: Thayer, 1992.

French, Esther, and Robert L. French. *The Griswold Family: The First Five Generations in America.* Wethersfield, CT: Griswold Family Association, 1990.

Goodwin, Nathaniel. *Genealogical Notes, or Contributions of the Family History of Some of the First Settlers of Connecticut and Massachusetts*. Boston: New England Historic Genealogical Society, 2013.

Griswold, Charlotte B. *Echoes Down the Valley: A Bicentennial Presentation*. Old Lyme, CT: Old Lyme Bicentennial Commission, 1976.

Griswold, Coralee, ed. *The Griswold Family: The Sixth and Seventh Generations, Edward and Matthew*. Vol. 1. Wethersfield, CT: Griswold Family Association, 2001.

Griswold, Earle A. *Malvern Hall*. Wethersfield, CT: Griswold Family Association, n.d.

Griswold, Evan. *An Ecological Inventory of Griswold Point Preserve*. Old Lyme, CT: The Nature Conservancy, Connecticut Chapter, 1975.

Griswold, John S. *Reflections*. Beverly, MA: Memoirs Unlimited, 1999.

Harned, William. "The History of the Griswold Manufacturing Company." www.cowtowncollectibles.com/Griswold%20History.htm.

Hayford, Harrison, ed. *The Journals of Herman Melville*. Evanston, IL: Northwestern University Press, 1989.

Heidler, D.S., and Jeanne T. Heidler. *Encyclopedia of the War of 1812*. Annapolis, MD: Naval Institute Press, 2004.

Heise, Gladys Lincoln. *History of Giant's Neck Beach, 1664–1923*. East Lyme, CT: Giant's Neck Beach Association, n.d.

Hurd, Hamilton D. *History of New London County, with Biographical Sketches of Its Prominent Citizens and Pioneers*. Philadelphia: J.W. Lewis and Company, 1882.

Kirk, Lydia Chapin. *Distinguished Service*. Syracuse, NY: Syracuse University Press, 2007.

Lamb, Martha J. *Lyme: A Chapter of American Genealogy*. Old Lyme, CT: Old Lyme Bicentennial Commission, 1976.

Lamb, Martha J., and Burton Harrison. *History of the City of New York: Its Origin, Rise and Progress*. Vol. 3. Reprint. New York: Cosimo Inc., 2005.

Landmarks of Old Lyme Connecticut. Old Lyme, CT: Ladies' Library Association, 1952.

Little, J. David. *Revolutionary Lyme: A Portrait, 1765–1783*. Supplement to the Annual Report of the Town of Old Lyme. Old Lyme, CT: Old Lyme Board of Finance, 1975.

Lubbock, Basil. *The Western Ocean Packets*. Mineola, NY: Dover Publications. 1988.

McBride, Rita M. "Roger Griswold: Connecticut Federalist." PhD diss. Yale University, 1948.

Morgan, James Morris. *Morgan's War: Volume 2—Recollections of a Rebel Reefer*. Tucson, AZ: Fireship Press, 1989.

"Olde Letters and Ye Histories of Firesides." *American Monthly Magazine* 5 (1894).

Pittsburgh Press. "Piano Company Is Out of Tune." August 23, 1901.

Riggins, Cleta. "Anna Wolcott Griswold." *Griswold Family Bulletin* 173 (June 2013).

Schavoir, Shelby, and Peter Schavoir. *John Sloane Griswold Ancestors and Descendants*. N.p.: self-published, 2004.

Stevens, Thomas A. *Old Lyme: A Town Inexorably Linked to the Sea*. Deep River, CT: Deep River Savings Bank, 1959.

Stitham, Norman. *Connecticut Regimental Histories: Old Lyme Civil War Volunteers, 1861–1865*. Old Lyme, CT: Old Lyme Historical Society, 2011.

Stone, John S. *Memoir of the Life of the Rt. Rev. Alexander Viets Griswold*. Philadelphia: Stavely and McCalla, 1845.

Storms, Robbi, and Don Malcarne. *Around Essex: Elephants and River Gods*. Charleston, SC: Arcadia Press, 2011.

Tucker, Phillip Thomas. *Burnside's Bridge: The Climactic Struggle of the 2ⁿᵈ and 20ᵗʰ Georgia at Antietam Creek*. Mechanicsburg, PA: Stackpole Press, 2000.

Twomey, Tom. *Discovering the Past: Writings of Jeanette Edwards Rattray, 1893–1974*. New York: Newmarket Press, 2001.

Wellejus, Edward. *Historic Erie County*. Erie, PA: Erie County Historical Society, 2003.

Weil, Francois. *Family Trees: A History of Genealogy in America*. Cambridge, MA: Harvard University Press, 2013.

Wilson, John. *Portrait Gallery of the Chamber of Commerce of the State of New York*. New York: New York Chamber of Commerce Press, 1890.

WEBSITES

www.florencegriswoldmuseum.org

www.oldtimeerieblogspot.com

www.politicalgraveyard.com

INDEX

ABOUT THE AUTHOR

Wick Griswold teaches the sociology of the Connecticut River Watershed at the University of Hartford's Hillyer College. He lives in Old Lyme, Connecticut.